Blacks in the United States Army

Portraits Through History

Blacks in the United States Army

Portraits Through History

Edited by MARTHA S. PUTNEY

McFarland & Company, Inc., Publishers
Jefferson, North Carolina, and London

LIBRARY OF CONGRESS CATALOGUING-IN-PUBLICATION DATA

Blacks in the United States Army : portraits through history /
edited by Martha S. Putney.
p. cm.
Includes bibliographical references and index.

ISBN 0-7864-1593-2 (illustrated case binding : 70# alkaline paper)

1. United States. Army — African American troops — History.
2. African American soldiers — History.
3. United States — History, Military.   I. Title.
E185.63 .B56 2003   355'.0089'96073 — dc21   2003006892

British Library cataloguing data are available

On the cover: A Study of a Negro Soldier, Color Sergeant W. H. Cox,
Reg't 369th Inf., N.Y.N.G., Champagne, France, 1918.
Raymond Desvarreaux. Oil, 24" × 15". West Point Museum Collections,
United States Military Academy at West Point, N.Y.

Manufactured in the United States of America

*McFarland & Company, Inc., Publishers
Box 611, Jefferson, North Carolina 28640
www.mcfarlandpub.com*

Dedicated to those blacks who have served
and are serving in the United States Army

and to the memory of my brother,
William H. Settle

Contents

Preface

The originals of the paintings, drawings, and sketches herein, except one in the family's possession, are in the public domain. More than 115 of them are from among more than 10,000 items in the Army Art Collection of the United States Army's Center of Military History. Others are from the collection of the West Point Museum at the United States Military Academy in West Point, New York, and the United States Air Force Art Collection. Six are from the Division of the Armed Forces History, National Museum of American History at the Smithsonian Institution.

Collectively, these portraits, accompanied by brief narratives, tell the story of blacks in the army from the Revolutionary War through the Persian Gulf War. These pictures, like others in the army's art collections, are historical paintings; they are a visual record of the men and women who served, and when and where they served.

Black army personnel are shown at war, as war casualties, at prayer, in peacetime assignments, in training, at play and at leisure, and as peacekeepers. In almost all of these instances, the artists' perceptions of the individual men and women are credible; the blacks have lifelike physical features.

This book is a commemoration of the service of African Americans in the United States Army.

The editor wishes to thank Marylou Gjernes, army art curator at the Center of Military History, for making available the files of the prints of the paintings. Verne E. Schwartz, director of the Image Resource Center of the United States Army Art Activity, was most helpful in assembling designated copies of the prints. My son read the introduction and the narratives and gave valuable suggestions.

1

Introduction

Blacks fought in most of the colonial wars and skirmishes. They fought in these engagements even though many of the colonies had laws, ordinances, or resolutions excluding them from the local militias. When the colonies faced an external foe, many of them permitted or encouraged or gave inducements to blacks to join in the fray. After the hostilities had ended and there was no longer a need for them, blacks were released from the militias.

The underlying reason for the legal exclusion of blacks from the militias was slavery: fear of slave revolts and rebellions; the possibility that non-slave blacks, if armed, would give aid to slaves and thus undermine the institution of slavery; and the stigma that race-based slavery had on non-slave blacks.

The Revolutionary War propaganda and the stirring words of the Declaration of Independence posited the coming of a new day for "all men." Blacks took up arms with the colonists at the beginning of the hostilities in Massachusetts. But it was not until after they had participated in two battles that the Massachusetts Committee of Safety adopted a resolution authorizing the recruitment of non-slave blacks for its militia. This resolution expressly barred the enlistment of slaves.

Some months later, in July 1775, George Washington, commander of the Continental Army, acting on a decision of the Council of War, announced that no blacks, non-slave or slave, were to be enrolled in the Continental Army. In October of the same year, the Council of War, possibly aware that blacks were among the fighting forces of the local militias, again declared that no blacks were to be enlisted. In November, George Washington issued a general order barring the recruitment of blacks.

However, a few days earlier, Lord Dunmore, the royal governor of Virginia, had issued a proclamation inviting blacks, both non-slave and slave, to join the royal army against the rebelling American colonists and promising freedom to those slaves who joined. Dunmore's proclamation caught the American patriots off-guard, and before the end of December 1775, George Washington reversed his position and approved the enlistment of non-slave blacks.

The following month, the Continental Congress recorded its approval of the enlistment.

At the time the Continental Congress acted, both the local militias and the Continental Army were plagued by a chronic shortage of troops since draft calls by the Congress were not met and short-term enlistments were a problem. Hence, Dunmore's proclamation was not the only incentive for the colonial government to change its policy. The simple need for more soldiers was a crucial factor in the decision to enlist blacks.

During the war, blacks served in the Continental Army and the militias of every state except South Carolina and Georgia, the only two states which did not authorize their enlistment. Most of the blacks who served were from the North. Virginia had more blacks in its militia than any other southern state. Some of these black soldiers were slaves who enrolled under the substitute system, taking the place of their holders, who, in many instances, promised them freedom after the completion of their term of service. This substitute system opened the door for the enlistment of slaves. Other slaves, without their holders' knowledge, also took up arms. Most of the black soldiers served in mixed units; others were in all-black units.

Blacks were also among the civilians who helped the war effort. They were laborers, messengers, spies, providers of food, and camp followers, and served other support roles. Among the camp followers were women who were mainly nurses, cooks, and laundresses.

Once the Revolutionary War had ended, the nation had gained its independence, and the government was established under the Constitution, Congress in 1792 enacted a law banning blacks from duty in the militias, for all practical purposes eliminating them from service in the United States Army. (The Marine Corps at its very beginning was prohibited by an act of Congress in 1798 from enlisting blacks. No such restriction was imposed on the Navy because of its chronic shortage of manpower.) This law of 1792 became the United States Army's official policy until 1862. The single exemption was for Louisiana, which, under promises made to the people of the territory at the time of its purchase, could opt out of the operation of laws which ran counter to the people's traditions and customs. Louisiana had permitted the existence of separate black militia units composed of free landowners.

The War of 1812 against England was in the main a naval war, but the army was also involved. During this war, most states refused to accept blacks in their militias, and the United States Army made no effort to enlist them. But they served. In the biggest land operation of the war, the Battle of New Orleans or the Battle on the Plains of Chalmette, the Louisiana Battalion of Free Men of Color and a battalion of black men from St. Domingo played a crucial role in the victory. Additionally, blacks provided menial support services for the army and answered the call for volunteers to shore up the coastal defenses in some states.

Despite the 1792 law and army regulations of 1820 and 1821 excluding blacks from the services, they participated on the United States' side in the Second Seminole War, and a significant number of them were on the battlefield during the Mexican War (1846–1848). Most of them were servants of the officers, who received government compensation for the work of their servants. These servants and other blacks performed a multitude of duties, both combat-support and combat. They were cooks, teamsters, stevedores, sanitary workers, stretcher bearers, nurses, couriers, drummer boys, and riflemen. Clearly they played an essential role in the ground war.

At the outset of the Civil War, neither President Lincoln nor the Congress had any intention of recruiting or enlisting blacks in the army. Indeed, blacks were rejected when they sought to volunteer. In large measure, this state of affairs existed because of the effect the black presence in the military would have had on the slave-holding border states, which the government wanted to remain loyal. (In the main, this war was about slavery.) But, again, battlefield need dictated a change. The Confiscation Act and the Militia Act of July 1862 opened the door for the official enlistment of a large body of blacks in the Union Army. Those blacks who enlisted or volunteered were organized as units of the United States Colored Troops (USCT) and were administered by the newly created War Department Bureau of Colored Troops.

The segregated USCT combat units, in many instances, fought side-by-side with their comrades-in-arms, led the charge of the attacking forces, or were a part of the reinforcement network. Most of the black units were organized into companies and regiments. One corps, the Twenty-fifth, was the only black corps in the history of the United States Army. (A corps is a large body of soldiers consisting of two or more divisions.) Black commissioned officers served with some of these units as company commander, platoon leader, chaplain, or surgeon.

As early as the autumn of 1862, black troops were engaged in battle with the Confederate forces. They fought in every important battle in 1864 and 1965. They were with General Grant when General Lee surrendered at Appomattox Court House on April 9, 1965.

During the course of the Civil War, blacks were among the victims at Fort Pillow (a Union outpost on the Mississippi River border) when it was captured by the Confederate troops, and at Andersonville (a Confederate prisoner-of-war camp in Georgia) where the rescued survivors were malnourished, emaciated, and weak. Some also were the victims of the "no quarters policy" in which the Confederate forces refused to accord blacks the status of soldiers when they were captured or defeated in battle. Even among their own comrades-in-arms, black troops were assigned a disproportionate amount of fatigue duty and heavy labor.

So widespread was this practice that some commanders received orders to distribute fatigue duties more equitably. Moreover, blacks had to wait until 1864 before pay equal to that received by non-blacks was authorized for them.

In this war, thousands of ex-slaves, most of them designated as contrabands, and other blacks aided the Union cause as laborers, cooks, nurses, laundresses, teamsters, guides, scouts, and spies.

After the Civil War, while some of the black troops were assigned to the southern states to support the restoration of loyal governments, Congress in 1866 authorized the War Department for the first time to accept blacks into the regular army (RA). As a result of this authorization, four units, the Ninth and Tenth Cavalry and the Twenty-fourth and Twenty-fifth Infantry Regiments, were formed and assigned to duty in the frontier territory in the West by 1869.

The men in these four units are known collectively as the Buffalo Soldiers. They were allotted inadequate equipment, broken-down horses, inferior rations, and passed-down clothing. They were discriminated against and, at times, were abused by the settlers in the frontier towns. Yet the Buffalo Soldiers did a remarkable job in advancing the settlement of the West.

The first three black graduates of the United States Military Academy at West Point — and hence the first black commissioned officers in the regular army (RA) — had brief tours of duty with the Buffalo Soldiers following their respective graduations in 1877, 1887, and 1889. As junior officers in an all non-black senior officer corps, Henry O. Flipper, John H. Alexander, and Charles Young were burdened by the then prevailing military traditions and the social customs and mores.

At the outbreak of the Spanish-American War, a number of states authorized the creation of black volunteer units to support the war effort. Some of these units had black officers. Charles Young, the only black West Point graduate then in the service (Flipper had been dismissed from the service and Alexander had died while serving as professor of military science and tactics at Wilberforce University) and at that time posted at Wilberforce, resigned from RA and joined the black Ninth Ohio Volunteer Infantry with the rank of major. However, only the Buffalo Soldiers were committed to combat.

At the end of the Spanish-American War, Young was released from volunteer service. He rejoined the RA and was sent to the Philippines where some units of the Buffalo Soldiers were assisting in the suppression of the Philippine independence movement.

The United States entered World War I in 1917 with the goal of making "the world safe for democracy." The trained and battle-tested Buffalo Soldiers, who had been patrolling the Mexican border and chasing Pancho Villa and his army, were kept in the West. (The army had cracked down harshly on some of the men in the Twenty-fifth Infantry and some of the Twenty-fourth Infantry when these men avenged their mistreatment by the townsfolk in Brownsville, Texas, in 1906 and in Houston, Texas, in 1917 respectively.) Charles Young, despite his display of physical fitness, was forced out of the army.

Amid demands of the black leaders, organizations, and the press for the commitment of black troops to combat, the War Department created two infantry divisions, the Ninety-second and the Ninety-third. The units of the Ninety-second Division were composed entirely of raw recruits or draftees, and those of the Ninety-third Division consisted of three National Guard companies and one company of draftees.

Neither of these infantry divisions was trained as a unit, neither was adequately trained, and neither had the normal divisional combat support forces. Once overseas, the Ninety-second became basically a labor division. Later, this division and the Ninety-third were assigned to the French army. With French training and weapons, and under French command, the various segments of the divisions had extensive combat duty, although they never fought as divisions.

After World War I had ended, the men in the divisions were discharged from the service and the divisions were deactivated. Only the Buffalo Soldier units remained in the army, but at significantly reduced strength. It was not until 1939, the year the German army marched into Poland, that the War Department began to increase its forces, which included several black units.

World War II was a truly global conflict. Its goals for the Allied Forces were set forth in the Four Freedoms: freedom of speech, freedom of religion, freedom from want, and freedom from fear. For its part, the United States had proclaimed itself the "arsenal of democracy." Despite the obvious inconsistency with democratic principles, the War Department retained its policy of racial segregation with its component of discrimination and its quota system by which the number of blacks in the service was not to exceed their percentage of the total population. Still within the quota, numerically more blacks were in the army than during any previous war. The Army Nurse Corps, which had permitted 18 black women to enroll in 1918 to help deal with the worldwide influenza epidemic, allowed some 500 of them to enroll, about 1 percent of the total strength of the corps. The Women's Army Auxiliary Corps / Women's Army Corps, which was created in 1942, permitted 6,500 black women to enroll, but never more than 4,040 were in the corps at any one time, a number representing less than 6 percent of the strength of the corps.

Just before the beginning of the Korean War, the quota system was abandoned, and proportionally more blacks were in the army and committed to combat than heretofore. During this war, black replacement troops were assigned to non-black units since they, unlike the black units, were understrength. This action was one of the first steps in the beginning of the desegregation of the army.

The army supplied its manpower needs for the Vietnam War, America's longest war, through the draft system. Percentage-wise, fewer blacks met the criteria for draft deferment, a determination made by the local draft boards. In 1972, the draft system was dropped and the all-volunteer army was instituted. This method of filling the ranks in the army resulted in the enrollment of a large number of blacks, many more than their percentage of the total population.

Significant numbers of blacks were in the service during the 1991 Persian Gulf War. By 1998, some 127,600 black men and women were in the army. In September 2000, they numbered 120,400 or 26.4 percent of the total enrollment.

In addition to the wars, black Americans were with the army when it assumed peacekeeping operations and other actions around the world. Peacekeeping operations took place in Europe as a part of the North Atlantic Treaty Organization (NATO); in Japan, the Philippines, and the Pacific Ocean islands after World War II; in South Korea after the Korean War; in the Middle East after the Persian Gulf War; in Macedonia in 1994 in Operation Able Sentry (to keep the Balkan War from spreading to that area); in Kuwait in 1994 to counter the aggressive forces in Iraq; in Bosnia in 1995 as a part of the NATO forces securing peace among the warring factions; and in the Sinai Desert since 1982 as part of the Multinational Force and Observers (MFO) to monitor the peace.

In other action, the army went into Grenada in 1983 in Operation Urgent Fury to prevent the emergence of a communist government, into Panama in 1989 in Operation Just Cause to depose a corrupt government, and into Haiti in 1994 in Operation Uphold Democracy to restore a democratically elected government. The army was a part of a United Nations force in Somalia in Operation Restore Hope in 1993–94 and in Rwanda in 1994 to help in relief efforts. On the home front, the army rendered assistance in such disasters as Hurricane Hugo in 1989, Hurricane Andrew in 1992, and the earthquake of California in 1994.

Revolutionary War
(1776–1783)

The First Rhode Island Regiment, an all-black unit, held off a combined British-Hessian charge long enough to enable an entire American army to escape a trap in the Battle of Rhode Island in August 1778. What made this feat

**1st Rhode Island Regiment, 29 August 1778. Jerry Pinkney, 1976. Watercolor, 30½" × 42½".
Courtesy of Army Art Collection, U.S. Army Center of Military History.**

noteworthy was that Rhode Island did not begin to recruit men for this regiment until June 1778 and, hence, the men were largely untrained when they met in battle. Subsequently, this regiment engaged the British in other battles including the one near Points Bridge in New York in 1781.

In the Revolutionary War, blacks fought in every major battle from the opening engagements at Lexington and Concord in Massachusetts in April 1775 to the British surrender at Yorktown in Virginia in October 1781. Blacks made up about 5,000 of the some 300,000 American troops who served in this war.

War of 1812
(1812–1814)

"George Latchom." This painting depicts a scene in which Latchom is participating in the Revolutionary War; however, he is included here because he also served in the War of 1812. Roy LaGrone, Minority Group Art Program, 1976. Watercolor on board, 30" × 42". Courtesy of Army Art Collection, U.S. Army Center for Military History.

The Louisiana Battalion of Free Men of Color offered its services to Andrew Jackson, the commanding officer of the American forces in New Orleans, who was preparing for an encounter with a numerically superior British army. This battalion and a company of black men from St. Domingue joined Jackson's army in the Battle of New Orleans, also known as the Battle of Chalmette Plains, in 1815. The black troops set up the perimeter defenses, held a strategic position, and confronted the advancing British forces. This battle was one of the few victories the Americans could celebrate after the war. Jackson commended the black soldiers for their valor and conduct and questioned the United States policy of excluding blacks from the military.

Earlier in this war, New York had authorized the recruitment of two black regiments, and Philadelphia had authorized a battalion of black troops to defend against the raids and incursions the British were making along the Atlantic coastline. But the war was over before either of theses two groups saw action. Additionally, more than 2,000 blacks responded to Philadelphia's call for the construction of a coastal defense network.

Most of the fighting in this war was on the seas with ship-to-ship and fleet-to-fleet combat.

Civil War (1861–1865)

In June 1863, Harriet Tubman led troops under the command of Colonel James Montgomery on a search and destroy mission in South Carolina in which supplies and property were seized or destroyed. Tubman served the Union Army as a spy, scout, guide, cook, and nurse throughout the war. Also, Susie King Taylor was the unofficial laundress and volunteer nurse for her husband's unit, the First South Carolina Volunteers, which became a unit of the United States Colored Troops. During her time with the unit, she taught the soldiers to read and write. She remained with the unit until the war's end. In addition, more than 200,000 other black civilians were involved in the Union war effort as nurses, laundresses, cooks, laborers, servants, guides, scouts, and spies.

The 54th Massachusetts Regiment, the first of the United States Colored Troops (USCT) units organized in the North, met its baptism of fire on July 18, 1863, at Fort Wagner, a fortified Confederate position at the entrance of Charleston Harbor in South Carolina. The 54th led the assault on the fort, met the deadly fire of the defenders, gained the parapet, entered the fort, and planted the regimental flag. But, because of the potent and persistent firepower of the defenders and the failure of the reinforcements to arrive to shore up its thinning ranks, the unit was ordered to retreat. The 54th had fought courageously.

Just two days prior to the assault on Fort Wagner, the 54th had engaged in skirmishes at the nearby James and Morris Islands and had entered the fray at Fort Wagner after a long forced march through heavy rain and horrendous weather.

During the course of the Civil War, black troops fought in more than 300 engagements and skirmishes including 35 major battles. They participated in the siege of Petersburg and of Richmond in 1864 and 1865 and were among the troops to enter these two cities when they were evacuated by the Confederate forces. They were present when Charleston was evacuated and were with General Grant when the Confederate General Robert E. Lee surrendered at Appomattox on April 9, 1965. Some 186,000 blacks served in the Union Army, about ten percent of the total enrollment. They suffered 68,000 casualties including 37,000 who lost their lives.

Above: Harriet Tubman, Civil War Period. Joan Bacchus Maynard, 1975. Oil on canvas, 36" × 30". *Opposite:* Action at Fort Wagner, 18 July 1863. Romare Bearden, 1975. Mixed media, 30" × 40". Courtesy of Army Art Collection, U.S. Army Center of Military History.

The Congressional Medal of Honor, the highest military award that can be bestowed on an individual, was authorized by Congress for soldiers in 1862 for bravery above and beyond the call of duty. The first blacks so honored were:

• Sergeant William H. Carney, who was born in Virginia in 1840 and migrated to Massachusetts, was a member of Company C, 54th Massachusetts Infantry Regiment. On July 18, 1853, during the assault on Fort Wagner, Carney rescued the regimental flag from a fallen comrade, led the attack on the walls of the fort, and planted the flag on the parapet. When the retreat was ordered under intense fire, Carney, with flag in hand, was hit in the hip and forced to crawl on one hand and one knee until he was assisted up. He was hit a second time and assisted up again. Badly wounded and suffering from loss of blood, he returned the flag to Union lines. He never once let the flag touch the ground.

• Sergeant Major Thomas R. Hawkins, who was born in Cincinnati, Ohio, was a member of the 6th USCT, which was engaged in battle at Deep Bottom, Virginia. Hawkins rescued the regimental flag during the action on July 21, 1864.

• Sergeant Decatur Dorsey, a native of Howard County, Maryland, and a member of Company B, 39th USCT, in the battle at Petersburg, Virginia, on July 30, 1864, placed the regimental colors on the Confederate's fortifications before his unit moved into position. When the regiment was forced back, Dorsey carried the colors and courageously rallied the men.

• Private William H. Barnes, who was born in St. Mary's County, Maryland, and was a member of Company C, 38th USCT, although wounded, was one of the first to enter the Confederate's fortifications in the battle at Chapin's Farm on September 29, 1964. (The fierce two-day struggle through woods and swamp at Chapin's Farm involved 13 black regiments and resulted in heavy casualties. More than 35 individuals received the Congressional Medal of Honor for their valor during this battle in Virginia.)

• First Sergeant Powhatan Beaty, a Richmond, Virginia, native and a member of Company G, 5th USCT, at Chapin's Farm, on September 29, 1864, took command of his company after all of the officers had been wounded or killed, and led it bravely.

• First Sergeant James H. Bronson, who was born in Indiana County, Pennsylvania, and was a member of Company D, USCT, took command of his company when all of the officers were wounded or killed, and led it valiantly on September 29, 1864 at Chapin's Farm.

• Sergeant Major Christian A. Fleetwood, a Baltimore, Maryland, native and 1858 graduate of what is now Lincoln University, was a member of the 4th USCT. On September 29, 1864, at Chapin's Farm, Fleetwood rescued the colors from two successive color bearers who had fallen, and carried them throughout the battle.

• Private James Gardiner, who was born in Gloucester, Virginia, was a member of Company I, 36th USCT. In the battle at Chapin's Farm on September 29, 1964, Gardiner ran ahead of his brigade, shot a Confederate officer who was standing on the parapet rallying the troops and then put him out of commission with a bayonet.

• Sergeant James H. Harris, a native of St. Mary's County, Maryland, and a member of Company B, 38th USCT, was honored for bravery in action at Chapin's Farm on September 29, 1864.

• Sergeant Alfred B. Hilton, a native of Harford County, Maryland, and a member of Company H, 4th USCT, took the regimental colors from a fallen comrade and carried them along with the national standard forward until he was wounded within enemy lines during the battle at Chapin's Farm on September 29, 1864.

• Sergeant Major Milton M. Holland, who was born in 1844 in Austin, Texas, assumed command of Company C after all of the officers were killed or wounded, and led it courageously at Chapin's Farm on September 29, 1964.

• Corporal James Miles was a member of Company B, 36th USCT. After his mutilated arm was amputated, James used his other hand to load and discharge his weapon in close quarters with the enemy, and at the same time urged his men forward at Chapin's Farm on September 29, 1864.

• First Sergeant Alexander Kelly, who was born in Pennsylvania and a member of Company F, 6th USCT, took the colors from a fallen comrade near enemy lines, and rallied his men to continue the fight when there was lack of direction at Chapin's Farm on September 29, 1864.

• First Sergeant Robert Pinn of Company I, 5th USCT, assumed command of his company when all of the officers were killed or wounded, and gallantly led it in battle at Chapin's Farm on September 29, 1864.

• First Sergeant Edward Ratcliff of Company C, 38th USCT, assumed command of his company after the commanding officer was killed, led it bravely, and was the first enlisted man to enter the enemy's fortifications at Chapin's Farm on September 29, 1864.

• Private Charles Veal of Company D, 4th USCT, seized the national colors after two successive color bearers had fallen close to enemy lines and carried the colors until the end of the battle at Chapin's Farm on September 29, 1864.

• Private Bruce Anderson, who was born on June 19, 1845, and a member of Company K of the 42nd New York Infantry Regiment, voluntarily advanced with the head of the company and cut down the palisade in the battle at Fort Fisher in North Carolina on January 15, 1965.

Frontier Wars
or Indian Wars
(1866–1890)

A CAMPFIRE SKETCH.

A Campfire Sketch, Sierra Bonitos, 1888. Frederic Remington. Pen and ink sketch. From the National Museum of American History, Smithsonian Institution, Military Collections.

Above: A Halt to Tighten the Packs, Arizona. Frederic Remington. Pen and ink sketch.
Below: Marching in the Desert, 10th Cavalry, Arizona, 1888. Pen and ink drawing. From the National Museum of American History, Smithsonian Institution, Military Collections.

A PULL AT THE CANTEEN.

A Pull at the Canteen, Arizona, 1888. Frederic Remington. Pen and ink sketch. From the National Museum of American History, Smithsonian Institution, Military Collections.

The men in the 24th and 25th Infantry Regiments and the 9th and 10th Cavalry, known as the Buffalo Soldiers, were the first blacks permitted to enlist in the Regular Army. They were sent to the West to patrol the vast expanse between the Mississippi River and the Rocky Mountains and between the Canadian border and the Mexican border. From 1866 to the 1890s, they battled the Indians,

Above: A Study in Action, Arizona. Frederic Remington. Pen and ink. *Opposite:* Marching on the Mountains. Frederic Remington. Pen and ink. Both from the National Museum of American History, Smithsonian Institution, Military Collections.

From Frederic Remington ("The Sign Language"). Frank Nicholas, 1970. Watercolor, 12½" × 16".

provided protection for the settlers and the mail, built roads and fortifications and camps, guarded the railroads under construction, tried to keep the peace between the settlers and the cattlemen, and pursued outlaws sometimes into Mexican territory. The Seminole Negro Indian Scouts, a small unit of black Seminole Indians, served with the Buffalo Soldiers at Fort Duncan and Fort Clark in Texas until they became disenchanted with the promises made to them by the army.

The Buffalo Soldiers engaged in pitched battles with the Comanche, Sioux, and Apache Indians and at times were ambushed by the Indians. They were involved in over a hundred clashes with Indians. They endured the racially hostile environment of some of the frontier towns and the social isolation and boredom of life on the frontier. They contributed significantly to the opening of the West for settlement.

Congressional Medal of Honor Recipients were:

• Sergeant Emanuel Stance, a member of Company F, 9th Cavalry, was cited for his leadership in forcing the Indian fighters to retreat and in repulsing their counterattack in action near Fort McKavett, Texas, in June 1870.

• Private Adam Paine, a Seminole Negro who was born in Florida, was commended for his brave action in Texas on September 26–27, 1874.

• Private Isaac Payne, a Seminole Negro Indian scout and a trumpeter who was born in Mexico, received his award for his commendable role in action at the Pecos River, Texas, on April 22, 1875.

• Private Pompey Factor, a Seminole Negro Indian scout who was born in Arkansas, was rewarded for his outstanding service at the Pecos River in Texas on April 25, 1875.

• Sergeant John Ward, a Seminole Negro Indian scout who was born in Mexico, was honored for his bravery in action at the Pecos River in Texas on April 25, 1875.

• Corporal Clinton Greaves, a native of Virginia and a member of Troop C, 9th Cavalry, was cited for his meritorious service in New Mexico on June 24, 1877.

• Sergeant John Denny, who was born in New York and was a member of Troop C, 9th Cavalry, received his award for action in fighting the Indians in New Mexico on September 18, 1879.

• Sergeant Thomas Boyne, a native of Maryland and a member of Troop C, 9th Cavalry, was cited for his bravery in action against the Indians in New Mexico on September 27, 1879.

- Sergeant Henery Johnson, who was born in Virginia and was a member of Troop D, 9th Cavalry, was honored for his bravery in action against the Indians on October 2–5, 1879, in Colorado.

- Sergeant George Jordan, a native of Tennessee and a member of Troop K, 9th Cavalry, received his medal for action against the Indians in New Mexico on August 12, 1881.

- Sergeant Thomas Shaw, who was born in Kentucky and a member of Troop K, 9th Cavalry, was cited for action in battle against the Indians in New Mexico on August 12, 1881.

- Private Augustus Walley, who was born in Maryland and a member of Troop I, 9th Cavalry, was honored for his action in fighting in New Mexico on August 16, 1881.

- First Sergeant Moses Williams, who was born in Louisiana and a member of Troop I, 9th Cavalry, received his medal for action against the Indians in New Mexico on August 16, 1881.

- Sergeant Brent Woods, a native of Kentucky and a member of Troop B, 9th Cavalry, was awarded the medal for action in battle on August 19, 1881, in New Mexico.

- Sergeant William McBryar, a native of North Carolina and a member of Troop K, 10th Cavalry, was rewarded for his brave action in battling the Indians in Arizona on March 7, 1889.

- Sergeant Benjamin Brown, who was born in Virginia and a member of Company B, 24th Infantry, was cited for meritorious action in battle on May 11, 1889, in Arizona.

- Corporal Isaiah Mays, a native of Virginia and a member of Company B, 24th Infantry, was cited for outstanding action in fighting against the Indians in Arizona on May 11, 1889.

- Corporal William O. Wilson, who was born in Maryland and a member of Troop I, 9th Cavalry, received his medal for bravery in the battles against Sioux Indians in 1890.

Spanish-American War (1898)

Charge of the First and Tenth Regular Cavalry. From sketches made at Las Guasimas, Cuba, 1898. Howard Chandler Christy. Tempera, 27" × 36". From the West Point Museum Collections, United States Miliary Academy, West Point, New York.

Private Thomas C. Butler, Cuba, 1898. Richard Dempsey, 1975. Oil on Canvas, 36" × 44".
Courtesy of Army Art Collection, U.S. Army Center of Military History. The soldier is
carrying a captured enemy flag amid the suffering and the dying.

At the outbreak of this ten-week war, Congress authorized a call for volunteers. Among those answering the call, four black units were organized. However, only the black regular army units, the 9th and 10th Cavalry and the 24th and 25th Infantry, whose combined strength was about 3,300 men, were committed to combat in Cuba. These units fought alongside of or reinforced other army units. The men in the black regular army units were crucial to American success in the battles at El Caney, Las Guasimas, and San Juan Hill. In the engagement at San Juan Hill, elements of the 9th and 10th Cavalry made possible the rout of Spanish forces by creating an opening in the enemy's defense. The 24th Infantry likewise saw action at San Juan Hill and the 25th Infantry and the 10th Cavalry battled at El Caney. Some of the men in the black units fought at Santiago and Tayabaca.

Negro Cavalry Provost Guard, Florida, 1898. Charles Johnson Post. Watercolor, 16½" × 22". Courtesy of Army Art Collection, U.S. Army Center of Military History. Florida was the staging area for troops en route to and returning from Cuba.

Six enlisted black men were given field promotions to the rank of second lieutenant for "meritorious service in the face of enemy action" in Cuba.

The stories of the Congressional Medal of Honor Recipients follow.

• Private Dennis Bell, a native of Washington, D.C., and a member of Troop H, 10th Cavalry, was cited for volunteering to go ashore under fire and helping to rescue wounded comrades on June 30, 1898, at Tayabaca, Cuba, after several other attempts had failed.

• Private Fitz Lee, who was born in Virginia and a member of Troop M, 10th Cavalry, was cited for volunteering to go ashore under fire and helping to rescue wounded comrades on June 30, 1898, at Tayabaca, Cuba, after several other attempts had failed.

• Private William H. Thompkins, who was born in New Jersey and was a member of Troop G, 10th Cavalry, was cited for volunteering to go ashore under fire and helping to rescue wounded comrades on June 30, 1898, at Tayabaca, Cuba, after several other attempts had failed.

• Private George H. Wanton, a native of New Jersey and a member of Troop M, 10th Cavalry, was honored for volunteering to go ashore under fire and helping to rescue wounded comrades on June 30, 1898, at Tayabaca, Cuba, after several other attempts had failed.

• Sergeant Major Edward L. Baker, who was born in Wyoming and was a member of the 10th Cavalry, was rewarded for leaving cover under fire and rescuing a wounded comrade from drowning at Santiago, Cuba, on July 1, 1898.

World War I (1914–1918)

The 369th Infantry Regiment, the federalized 15th Infantry Regiment of the New York National Guard, was under fire for 191 days in both offensive and defensive action and reportedly never lost ground to the enemy. It was the first unit of the Allied Forces to reach the Rhine River. At one point, in one sector of the war zone, the 369th was the only defense between the German army and Paris. Dubbed the "Hell Fighters," the regiment captured more than 400 Germans and killed or wounded many others while almost 200 of its men were killed in action and more than 800 others were wounded. None of its men was captured and one, Private Henry Johnson, almost single-handedly killed, wounded, or routed a 25-member German attacking party. The 369th, reportedly, was regarded as one of the most efficient units of the Allied Forces. The unit, a part of the 93rd Division which fought separately under the French command, was awarded two Croix de Guerre by the French for action on two sectors of the front, and individual members were awarded the Croix de Guerre and the Legion of Honor Medal for their heroic deeds.

The 370th Infantry Regiment of the 93rd Division, the federalized 8th Illinois Regiment of the National Guard, fought on several sectors of the front including St. Mihiel and the Argonne Forest. Fighting with French units, the 370th helped to drive the enemy out of France and fought in the last battle of the war. The other two regiments of the 93rd Division, the 371st and the 372nd Infantry, were in combat on several sectors of the front. Additionally, the 372nd pursued the retreating Germans. Together, these two regiments captured several hundred

Illustrations on the following two pages: (Left, page 32) **Full Length Study of Corp. C. Thompson, 15th Inf. A.E.F. WWI, Wearing Full Field Pack, Champagne, France, 1918.** Raymond Desvarreaux. Oil, 24" × 15". (Right, page 33) **A Study of a Negro Soldier, Color Sergeant W. H. Cox, Reg't 369th Inf., N.Y.N.G., Champagne, France, 1918.** Raymond Desvarreaux. Oil, 24" × 15". Both from West Point Museum Collections, United States Military Academy at West Point, N.Y.

C. CLARKE BUGLER
15ᵗʰ New York Infantry

Champagne 1918

Raymond Desvarreu
S'amarin 1918
(Alsace)

prisoners-of-war and large quantities of enemy equipment and supplies. Both of these regiments were cited by the French for gallantry and awarded the Croix de Guerre, as were some individuals of the units.

The other division committed to combat was the 92nd, which was composed entirely of draftees. The division's units, the 365th, 366th, 367th and 368th Infantry Regiments, fought separately under French command in the St. Die Metz sectors of the front and in several other areas. They also participated in day and night patrols and raiding parties. Some units of this division came under heavy artillery attacks and some were exposed to gas. The men in the 92nd Division faced a mounting toll of casualties: more than 670 men were gassed and about 800 others were wounded or killed in action. The grateful French government bestowed awards on many of the men in this division.

The combined strength of the 92nd and 93rd Divisions was about 42,000 of the some 400,000 black servicemen in the army during the war. The rest of them were assigned to service or labor units. These men were the stevedores, the teamsters, the laborers, the depot workers, and the service aides. They did a fantastic job of loading, unloading, and moving hundreds of thousands of tons of materiel, equipment, and supplies from the ships to the depots and thence to the combat areas. Some performed menial tasks stateside, dockside, and in combat-support areas.

The army kept the four black regular army units, its only battle-tested and experienced black troops, stateside where they engaged Pancho Villa and patrolled the Mexican border. Colonel Charles Young, the highest-ranking black regular army officer, was forced out of the service during the war years despite his protest of physical readiness.

Congressional Medal of Honor Recipient:

• Corporal Freddie Stowers of South Carolina was cited for bravery in leading his company in a charge on a German-held hill in France on September 28, 1918. Stowers and some 80 of his 200-man company paid the supreme price for their effort. (Although Stowers was recommended for the medal in December 1918, it was not approved until April 1991 after years of prodding and a lengthy review of the records.)

Opposite: Full Length Study of Negro Soldier, Bugler C. Clarke, 15th N.Y. Infantry 1918, with Full Field Pack and Bugle, Champagne, France, 1918. Raymond Desvarreaux. Oil, 34"×14". From West Point Museum Collections, United States Military Academy at West Point, N.Y.

World War II
(1941–1945)

Normandy Victory Cargo World War II, England, 1944. Lawrence Beall Smith. Oil on Masonite, 19½" × 23¾". Courtesy of Army Art Collection, U.S. Army Center of Military History. Some of the wounded are evacuated from the "D-Day" invasion of France at Normandy on June 6, 1944, and a beachhead is established.

Evacuating Wounded Soldier, England, June 1944. Harrison Standley. Watercolor, 15½" × 22⅜". Courtesy of Army Art Collection, U.S. Army Center of Military History. "Stretcher bearers of a medical battalion carry a casualty from the hold of an LST to a waiting ambulance which will take them to a nearby field hospital. The LST has just returned from Normandy bringing about 300 ambulatory casualties and about 30 stretcher cases. Seamen from the LST's and soldiers about to embark for France watch with interest. On board the evacuating LST's the cases are cared for by Navy medical personnel."—Harrison Standley

More than a million blacks were in the army during World War II and about one-half of them were sent overseas. More than three-fourths of all blacks in the army were in service and supply units. Most of them were in the quartermaster and transportation corps, and others were in the engineer, signal, medical, and other service branches. They were the stevedores who loaded and unloaded ammunition and vast quantities of other equipment, materiel, and supplies. They transported troops, ammunition, and supplies. They were the stretcher-bearers, ambulance drivers, gravediggers, orderlies, and the cooks and bakers. They cleared away obstacles, set up camps, and constructed roads, airstrips, airfields, and buildings. Still others were janitors, guards, mechanics, and ammunition handlers.

Waiting for the Wounded, Normandy, 1944. Harrison Stanley. Watercolor, 10″ × 13¾″. Courtesy of Army Art Collection, U.S. Army Center of Military History. "Negro ambulance drivers and stretcher bearers of a Medical Battalion wait on the beach to unload the wounded from LST's which have evacuated them from the Normandy beachhead. The wounded, during the first week of the invasion, were landed on the beaches in many cases to avoid congestion around the yards and docks where supplies and men were being sent to France."— Harrison Standley

They were organized as port battalions, engineer construction units, medical corpsmen, and labor units or battalions. The Second Cavalry Division, originally created to serve in the European Theater of Operations, was sent to Africa. Once there, it was disbanded and its personnel was formed into labor units.

About 500 black females were permitted to enroll in the Army Nurse Corps. They were assigned to army hospitals in the States and some worked in field hospitals in Liberia, England, Australia, New Guinea, and the Philippines. Black doctors and dentists also served in the States and overseas. Additionally, some 6,500 black women enrolled in the Women's Army Auxiliary Corps / Women's Army Corps. A majority of these enrolled women worked in army hospitals. Others were clerks, truck drivers, messengers, cooks, technicians, recruiting

Above: Night Shift, Italy, World War II. Joseph Hirsch, 1944. Oil, 27⅜″ × 37½″. *Below:* Elegy in New Guinea Graveyard, Port Moresby, 1943. Sidney Simon. Oil on Canvas, 20⅛″ × 25″. Both courtesy of Army Art Collection, U.S. Army Center of Military History.

Above: Hoisting Supplies from the Hold, England, 1944. Manuel Bromberg. Charcoal on Paper, 16" × 19½". *Below:* Cargo Ship, Canion Island, Pacific, 1943. Paul Sample. Oil on Canvas, 22" × 32". Both courtesy of Army Art Collection, U.S. Army Center of Military History.

Above: At a Supply Depot in England, 1943. Olin Dows. Watercolor, 11⅝" × 17¼". *Below:* Breaking Camp, Alaska, 1943. Joe Jones. Pastel on Paper, 13½" × 19½". Both courtesy of Army Art Collection, U.S. Army Center of Military History.

Above: Outdoor Service Station, England, 1943. Albert Gold. Ink and Watercolor, 21⅛" × 29½". *Below:* Checking Headlights, England, 1944. Albert Gold. Watercolor on Paper, 21" × 29¼". Both Courtesy of Army Art Collection, U.S. Army Center of Military History.

Above: Off to Work, England, 1943. Albert Gold. Watercolor and Ink, 21⅛" × 29½". *Below:* Engineer Equipment, England, 1943. Albert Gold. Crayon on Paper, 10" × 16". Both courtesy of Army Art Collection, U.S. Army Center of Military History.

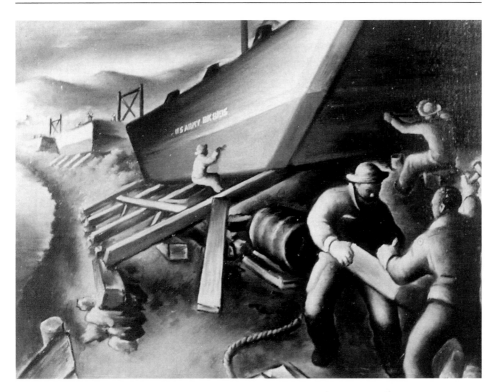

Above: Barge Building, England, 1944. David Lax. Oil on Canvas, 27" × 34". *Below:* Guarding Supplies, Italy, 1944. Tom Craig. Watercolor on Paper, 15" × 22½". Both courtesy of Army Art Collection, U.S. Army Center of Military History.

Above: Dusty Road, New Guinea, 1943. Barse Miller. Watercolor on Paper, 10" × 13⅛".
Below: Messmen Inspecting T.B.F., WW II USS Ranger, 1943. Paul Sample. Watercolor on Paper, 14" × 20". Both courtesy of Army Art Collection, U.S. Army Center of Military History.

Dinghow, China, 1944. John G. Hanlen. Ink, 9½" × 7½". Courtesy of Army Art Collection, U.S. Army Center of Military History.

Army Cook, Alaska, 1943. Joe Jones. Oil, 26" × 36". Courtesy of Army Art Collection, U.S. Army Center of Military History.

Above: Troops Cooking in the Open, England, 1943. Albert Gold. Watercolor on Paper, 21⅛" × 29½". "This is a typical scene at an American Army camp in England. Over this stove in the open air, these cooks are preparing a meal and keeping warm. The GI cans contain water to be used in washing mess kits after the meal."— Albert Gold. *Below:* Late Afternoon in the Mess Hall, Ireland, 1943. Albert Gold. Watercolor on Paper, 21½" × 29". Both courtesy of Army Art Collection, U.S. Army Center of Military History.

Above: Negro Soldiers Talking on Deck, England, 1943. Olin Dows. Ink on Paper, 12⅞" × 20⅝". *Below:* Negro Troops Playing Cards on Deck, England, 1944. Olin Dows. Watercolor, 13" × 19¾". Both courtesy of Army Art Collection, U.S. Army Center of Military History.

Chow Line, Alaska, 1943. Joe Jones. Gouache, 15" × 21½". Courtesy of Army Art Collection, U.S. Army Center of Military History.

assistants, and band members. In early 1945, a battalion of these women consisting of some 830 was sent to the European Theater of Operations to move a gigantic backlog of mail.

UNITS IN COMBAT AND COMBAT-SUPPORT ACTION

Two divisions and several smaller black units were committed to ground combat action during the war. The 92nd Division, known as the Buffalo Division, with more than 10,000 men in its various units and no black field grade officers, was sent in segments to the Mediterranean combat area beginning in July 1944. It fought in the Italian campaign, yet never as a unit until near the end of the campaign, and without a full complement of combat support forces. Despite some negative official reports, the various segments of the division accomplished their assigned missions. Individuals in the division were awarded more than 60 Silver Stars, two Distinguished Service Crosses, and over 1,000 Purple

Life and Death — Landing Operation Synthesis #9, Arawe, 1944. David Fredenthal. Watercolor, 21″ × 29½″. Courtesy of Army Art Collection, U.S. Army Center of Military History.

Hearts. The Italian government bestowed on the division the Military Cross for Merit for its valiant action against the enemy. Almost 3,000 of the men in the division were killed or wounded in action.

The 93rd Division was sent in segments to the Pacific Theater of Operations beginning in April 1944. It never fought as a unit and, like the 92nd Division, it never had a full complement of combat support forces nor black field-grade officers. Unlike the 92nd Division, the 93rd saw very little combat duty. In the main, the men were assigned to patrol duty, the unloading or loading of ships, or other non-combat duties. Some units in the division engaged the enemy in Bougainville and others were involved in clean-up operations. More than 580 of the division's men were killed in action and 2,580 others were wounded.

Among the less than division-size units was the 320th Anti-Aircraft Barrage Balloon Battalion, which participated in the "D-Day" invasion at Normandy, France. A trucking outfit and some quartermaster units gave support in France

Sergeant Gives Order, Guadalcanal, 1943. Aaron Bohrod. Oil, 21¼" × 17". Courtesy of Army Art Collection, U.S. Army Center of Military History.

Above: K-Rations, Bastogne, Belgium, 1945. Aaron Bohrod. Oil, 17" × 24". *Below:* Four Soldiers, Alaska, 1943. Joe Jones. Watercolor, 14½" × 21½". Both courtesy of Army Art Collection, U.S. Army Center of Military History.

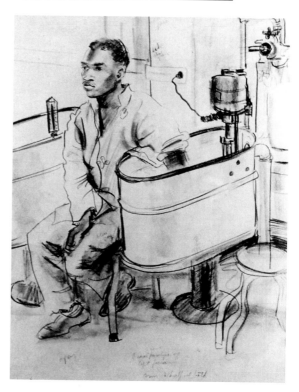

Above: Negro Soldier, The Pacific, 1943. Aaron Bohrod. Gouache, 14" × 12⅞". *Right:* Whirlpool Bath, Radial Paralysis of Left Arm, Atlantic City, New Jersey, 1944. Marion Greenwood. Crayon on Paper, 24" × 19". *Below:* Radio Man, Italy, 1945. Ludwig MacTarian. Gouache, 13" × 15¼". All courtesy of Army Art Collection, U.S. Army Center of Military History.

Advanced Reconditioning Pully Exercises for Injured and Paralyzed Limbs, England General Hospital, New Jersey, 1944. Marion Greenwood. Pencil on Paper, 17¾" × 12". Courtesy of Army Art Collection, U.S. Army Center of Military History. The wounded were treated at field hospitals overseas and then sent to Army General Hospitals in the States for further treatment and reconditioning.

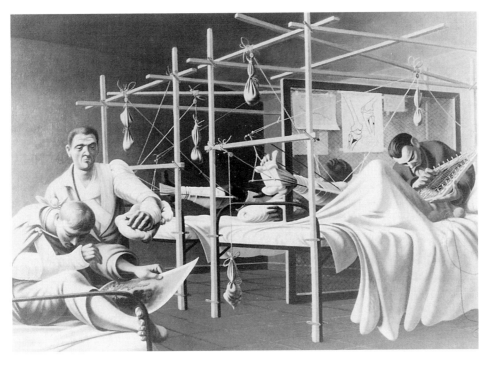

Above: Fracture Ward, New York, 1944. Peter Blume. Oil on Canvas, 24⅛″ × 36¼″. *Below:* Volleyball Game: Advanced Reconditioning, Patients Class II. Marion Greenwood. Watercolor, 12″ × 18″. Both courtesy of Army Art Collection, U.S. Army Center of Military History.

Above: 1st Class Passenger, Hospital Train, World War II. Robert Benney. Watercolor, 10"
× 10½". *Opposite, top:* Baseball, New Hebrides, 1943. Aaron Bohrod. Gouache on Paper,
14" × 19". *Bottom:* A Good Joke, Alaska, 1943. Joe Jones. Pastel on Paper, 12½" × 18½". All
courtesy of Army Art Collection, U.S. Army Center of Military History.

Above: Street in Noumea — Off Duty, Noumea, New Caledonia, 1943. Aaron Bohrod. Gouache on Paper, 13" × 24½". *Opposite:* Real Cool Harmony, Alaska, 1943. Joe Jones. Gouache on Paper, 19" × 13". Both courtesy of Army Art Collection, U.S. Army Center of Military History.

where it engaged the Germans. Also, the 1698th Engineer Combat Battalion aided the Allied Army's advance in the Ruhr Valley.

The most commended of the black ground forces was the 761st Medium Tank Battalion. This battalion participated in the Battle of the Bulge, considered by some historians as "the biggest battle the United States Army ever fought." It battled a numerically superior German armored unit at the latter's base in Belgium, broke through the Siegfried Line, knocked out German fortifications in several towns, and opened the way for the Allied Forces to enter Germany. It was engaged in battle for 183 continuous days, ending its mission on May 6, 1945, two days before the end of the war in Europe.

In the course of its operations, the 761st captured more than 450 German vehicles and ammunition trucks. The men in the unit received more than ten Silver Stars, 60 Bronze Star Medals, and almost 300 Purple Hearts. Between 1945 and 1976, the unit was nominated six times for the Presidential Unit Citation for Extra-ordinary Heroism, which was finally bestowed in 1978. The 761st was the only black unit so honored for its combat duty during World War II. After the cessation of hostilities in Europe, the 761st was assigned as a part of the Army of Occupation there.

ARMY AIR CORPS

During World War II, the army commissioned more than 900 black pilots and trained hundreds of technical and administrative specialists, mechanics, and other support personnel. Known as the Tuskegee Airmen, these individuals were organized into four groups: the 99th Fighter Squadron, the 332nd Fighter Group (composed of three squadrons), the 477th Bombardment Group, and the 553rd Fighter Replacement Training Squadron.

The first two units, the 99th Fighter Squadron and the 332nd Fighter Group, consisting of about 450 officers and their support personnel, were assigned to the European Theater of Operations for combat duty. The 99th Fighter Squadron flew its first combat mission in June 1943. During its existence, it gave air support to the ground fighting in North Africa, in the battle of Sicily, in the invasion of Italy, in the Anzio beachhead, in the Rome-Arno sector, in the Po Valley, in the Rhineland, and in the Allied Army's advance on other enemy strongholds in Italy and Southern France. In one display of extraordinary proficiency, the pilots of the 99th downed five enemy planes within a time frame of five minutes. As a separate entity, the squadron was awarded three Distinguished Unit Citations.

In July 1944, the 99th Fighter Squadron was made a part of the 332nd Fighter Group, which had been in combat since January 1944. The 332nd Fighter Group carried out missions in the Rome-Arno sector, in southern and northern France, in Rhineland, in Romania, in Greece, in the Balkans, in Poland, in Austria, and in the various other locations in Germany where Allied troops were committed. The fighter group escorted and protected bombers and engaged in aerial combat with enemy aircraft. Its men were credited with having been the only Allied escort group which never lost a bomber to enemy aircraft. Two of the group's pilots are credited with knocking out a German destroyer, a feat no other pilot or pilots had accomplished. The group as a whole received a Distinguished Unit Citation.

The Tuskegee Airmen were engaged in over 1,550 missions including more than 15,550 sorties. They destroyed or damaged some 400 enemy aircraft, 30 barges or boats, 20 buildings, 120 locomotives, 600 boxcars or rolling stock, 12 power transformers and radar installations, three gun emplacements, two oil and ammunition dumps, and a naval destroyer.

A Few of the Lonely Eagle. Terry Emerson, 1980. Courtesy of United States Air Force Art Collection. Benjamin O. Davis, Jr., was the commanding officer of both the 99th Fighter Squadron and the 332nd Fighter Group. The Tuskegee Airmen are sometimes referred to as the Lonely Eagle. (The Air Corps was a part of the Army during World War II.)

In recognition of their exploits, individual members of the 99th Fighter Squadron and the 332nd Fighter Group were awarded 150 Distinguished Flying Crosses, a Legion of Merit, a Silver Star, eight Purple Hearts, 14 bronze Stars, 744 Air Medals and Clusters, and a Silver Medal. Sixty-six of the Tuskegee Airmen were killed in action and more than 30 others were killed during training flights or in routine missions.

During World War II, blacks were involved in virtually every branch of the army and in every sector of the war, some in combat and others in non-combat roles. In addition to the involvement noted above, an amphibious trucking unit and two port companies landed at Iwo Jima with the marines. They were among the American troops in Australia and the labor units that constructed the Burma-Ledo Road and the road through Canadian territory to Alaska.

Periodic calls for a review of the records to ascertain whether any blacks were deserving of the Congressional Medal of Honor led the army in 1993 to support a federally funded study. After a careful examination of the documents, the findings of the research team were submitted to a special Army Senior Officer Awards Board, which recommended seven individuals for the Congressional Medal of Honor. Six of these men had previously received the Distinguished Service Cross, the second highest military honor, and the other had been awarded the Silver Star.

In presenting the nation's highest military honor to the one survivor, Vernon J. Baker, and the next-of-kin of the other six on January 13, 1997, President William J. Clinton said that "history has been made whole" for these men. Following are the stories of the seven recipients.

• Private George Watson was a resident of Birmingham, Alabama, and a member of the 29th Quartermaster Regiment. On March 8, 1943, Japanese bombs badly damaged a transport ship with Watson aboard near Forloch Harbor, New Guinea. With the vessel sinking and an order given to abandon ship, Watson stayed in the water to help those who could not swim to life rafts. Exhausted by his efforts, Watson was caught in pull of the sinking ship. He disappeared in the waters and his body was not recovered.

• Staff Sergeant Ruben Rivers had lived in Tecumseh, Oklahoma, and was a member of Company A, 761st Tank Battalion, 3rd Army. Rivers had refused

Opposite: **General Daniel Chappie James. Terry Emerson, 1976. Courtesy of United States Air Force Art Collection. Daniel James, Jr., was commissioned in the Army Air Corps in July 1943, but was not among those sent overseas. Peter C. Verwayne and Charles R. Stanton, two of the individuals pictured at the bottom of the painting, were replacement pilots in the 332nd Fighter Group. In 1975, as a member of the United States Air Force, Daniel James became the first black four-star general in the military forces. (The Air Corps was a part of the Army during World War II.)**

medication and evacuation after his tank hit a German mine in France. Despite a severely cut leg, Rivers took charge of another tank and continued to fight. Three days later, on November 19, 1944, near the town of Bourgal-troff, when the lead tank of his battalion met with antitank fire, Rivers radioed that he was going to pursue the enemy after he was ordered to retreat. In the ensuing engagement, a German shell hit his tank and fatally wounded him. (River's non-black commanding officer, David Williams, who is still alive at this writing, maintains that he gave his commanding officer a written recommendation for a Medal of Honor for Rivers. No record has been found of this recommendation. Over time, Williams has continued to pursue recognition for the unit and for Rivers.)

• First Lieutenant Charles L. Thomas was a resident of Detroit, Michigan, and the commanding officer of Company C, 614th Tank Destroyer Battalion, 103rd Division. He volunteered on December 14, 1944, to lead a tank platoon to draw fire and to serve as a decoy for a combined armored and infantry attack on the enemy. At Climbach, near the German border, the platoon and Thomas's armored scout car were attacked. The windows and tires were shot out of his scout car. Wounded, Thomas mounted the top of the car and machine-gunned the enemy. Hit again on the arms, legs, and chest, Thomas got under the vehicle where he continued to fight and direct the firepower of his troops' antitank guns at the enemy. He refused to accept medical evacuation until his troops were positioned to continue the fighting.

• First Lieutenant John R. Fox was a resident of Boston, Massachusetts, and an artillery observer with Cannon Company, 366th Infantry Regiment, 92nd Division. Fox volunteered to establish a forward observation post in a house in Sommocolonia, Italy, where some 1,000 men of the 92nd Division were dispatched on a thirty-mile front to combat the enemy. Thinly spread across the terrain, the men of the 92nd were met by a superior force of German and Italian soldiers on December 26, 1944. Fox radioed for artillery fire to be directed in part of his observation post while the 92nd men were withdrawing. Knowing that the artillery fire would rain on Fox, the command post hesitated to take action until a second call came from Fox and permission was given by officers up the chain of command. Later, Fox's body was recovered where there were more than 100 bodies of the enemy.

• Staff Sergeant Edward A. Carter, Jr., had lived in Los Angeles, California, and was a member of Provisional Infantry Company No. 1, 56th Armored Infantry, 12th Armored Division. On March 23, 1945, Carter volunteered to

Opposite: Observation Pilot, Viareggio, Italy. Ludwig Mactarian, 1945. Gouache, 15¼" × 9¾". Courtesy of Army Art Collection, U.S. Army Center of Military History.

lead a three-man patrol across an open field near Speyer, Germany, toward a warehouse from which the enemy had fired on his rifle squad's tanks. After one of his men was killed by small arms fire, Carter ordered the other two to move to safety and provide cover for him. Before they could gain safer ground, a second one was killed and the third was wounded. Carter himself sustained wounds to the leg, the arm, and the hand before he reached the warehouse. Once there, he waited behind some earthwork for the enemy to appear. Of the eight who came in sight, Carter killed six of them and used the others as a shield to return to his squad.

• Second Lieutenant Vernon J. Baker of St. Maries, Idaho, was a platoon leader of Company C, 370th Infantry Regiment, 92nd Division. On April 5, 1945, Baker led his platoon against a German artillery attack in a mountain stronghold in Italy near Castle Aghinolfi. Baker killed two German soldiers inside a bunker, took out a camouflaged machine gun nest along with two more enemy soldiers, and killed a retreating soldier who had tossed a hand grenade that failed to explode after hitting the helmet of his non-black company commander. Baker then moved on a second dugout where he found two more German soldiers and killed them. Before the encounter ended, Baker directed fire toward himself to permit the evacuation of his wounded men. Only seven of Baker's twenty-five-man platoon survived the ordeal; Baker was wounded in the hand. Altogether, Baker's platoon had killed 26 enemy soldiers, took out six machine gun nests, put out of commission two observation posts, and overran four dugouts.

• Private First Class Willy F. James, Jr., of Kansas City, Kansas, was a member of Company G, 413th Infantry Regiment, 104th Division. On April 7, 1945, when his regiment wanted to secure the crossing of a bridge over the Weser River, James volunteered to scout ahead of his platoon to observe enemy positions. On his return to report his observations, he drew fire. His platoon leader was hit, and when James went to the aid of the platoon leader, both were fatally wounded.

Korean War
(1950–1953)

On July 21, 1950, about one month after the outbreak of hostilities, the all-black 24th Infantry Regiment, which had been stationed in Japan, won the first battlefield victory in the war. Later, this regiment was criticized for inefficiency.

Technically, this was a United Nations war, but the United States contributed about 90 percent of the military effort. Since the quota system had been dropped, the military depended on the draft system with its built-in deferment policy to fill its ranks. As a result, more blacks were inducted into the military. Hence, black

Mass in the Field. B. Keeler. Oil, 38" × 50". Courtesy of Army Art Collection, U.S. Army Center of Military History.

replacement troops exceeded the number needed for black units and a military decision was made to assign the excess black replacement soldiers to under-strength non-black units. (President Truman had since the end of World War II been urging the military to integrate.)

Before the end of the Korean War, blacks made up more than 13 percent of the strength of the army, and more than 40 percent of the some 300,000 blacks in the army were committed to combat duty. Also, for the first time, blacks held field grade officer rank in Korea.

Congressional Medal of Honor Recipients:

• Private First Class William Thompson, who was born in New York and a member of Company M, 24th Infantry Regiment, 25th Infantry Division, was cited for bravery in battle near Haman, Korea, on August 6, 1950, when he single-handedly held off a surprise attack of a large enemy force under cover of darkness long enough to permit his platoon to move to safer ground. He was mortally wounded by enemy fire as he continued to man his machine gun.

• Sergeant Cornellus H. Charlton, a native of West Virginia and a member of Company C, 24th Infantry Regiment, 25th Infantry Division, was honored for heroic action in battle near Chipo-ri, Korea, on June 2, 1951, when he assumed leadership of his platoon after the platoon leader was wounded, and led a charge on a hill. On the third charge, after heavy casualties, Charlton and his men gained control of the hill and dislodged the enemy. Twice hit by enemy fire, 22-year-old Sergeant Charlton died of his wounds.

Vietnam War
(1960–1973)

Over 16,500 blacks were committed to combat before the end of 1965 in this conflict, America's longest war. As the war continued, their numbers increased. They comprised more than 14 percent of all the servicemen in the war zone and an even larger percentage of those in combat units.

They were in virtually every arm and service of the army. They, with their comrades-in-arms, conducted search and destroy missions. They were often attacked under the cover of darkness, caught in ambushes, and pinned down by an unseen enemy. They were among the prisoners-of-war and the missing-in-action. A significant number of them were among the more than 55,000 killed-in-action.

Regarding the Congressional Medal of Honor Recipients, black commissioned officers were among the recipients for the first time since the medal was authorized.

• Private First Class Milton L. Olive, III, of Chicago, a member of the 3rd Platoon, Company B, 2nd Battalion (Airborne), 503rd Infantry, 173rd Airborne Brigade, was on a search and destroy mission on October 25, 1965, in the jungle in Phu Cuong to clear out the Viet Cong from the area when his platoon encountered heavy enemy fire and reacted. The fleeing Viet Cong threw a grenade in the midst of the men and Olive grabbed it and fell on it and thereby sacrificed himself and saved the lives of the other members of his platoon. Olive was 18 years old when he was killed in action.

• Specialist Fifth Class Laurence Joel, a native of Winston-Salem, North Carolina, moved quickly on November 8, 1965, to care for the men wounded in the forward squad when a large Viet Cong force launched a surprise attack from a concealed position. He proceeded to attend to others as the unit moved forward. Although twice wounded by bullets hitting all around him, Joel, a medical-aid man, continued his mission of mercy by dragging

Jungle trail. Robert B. Rigg. Oil, 20" × 24". Courtesy of Army Art Collection, U.S. Army Center of Military History.

Jungle Column, 15th Battalion, 28th Infantry Division, Vietnam, 1967. Samuel E. Alexander. Watercolor, 15½" × 22⅛". Courtesy of Army Art Collection, U.S. Army Center of Military History.

Above: Rifleman, Vietnam, 1969. James S. Hardy. Ink on Paper, 16" × 18". *Opposite:* Scout Dogs, Vietnam, 1966. Ronald E. Pepin. Watercolor on paper, 11¾ × 9". Both courtesy of Army Art Collection, U.S. Army Center of Military History.

Above: Grenadier, Vietnam, 1967. William Linzee Prescott. Watercolor on Paper, 11¾" × 8⅞". *Opposite:* Member of 1st Air Cavalry on a Search and Destroy Mission, Vietnam, 1967. Peter Copeland. Watercolor on Paper, 14" × 11". Both courtesy of Army Art Collection, U.S. Army Center of Military History.

Rifleman, Vietnam, 1968. John D. Kurtz. Pencil, 11" × 9". Courtesy of Army Art Collection, U.S. Army Center of Military History.

Left: Cavalry Trooper, Vietnam, 1968. John D. Kurtz. Watercolor on Paper, 9" × 11½". *Below:* Gunner's Eye View, Vinh Long, Vietnam, 1967. Kenneth J. Scowcroft. Pencil, 18½" × 19½". Both courtesy of Army Art Collection, U.S. Army Center of Military History.

Ready for Patrol wth the 173 Airborne Brigade, Ben Song, Vietnam, 1969. Jack O'Hara. Pencil on Board, 10" × 15". Courtesy of Army Art Collection, U.S. Army Center of Military History.

Right: Tank Driver, Vietnam, 1968. John D. Kurtz. Watercolor, 12" × 9". *Below:* Waiting, Vietnam, 1967. Daniel Lopez. Watercolor on Board, 15" × 19". Both courtesy of Army Art Collection, U.S. Army Center of Military History.

Four Deuces, Vietnam, 1973. William F. Voiland. Acrylic, 42" × 30". Courtesy of Army Art Collection, U.S. Army Center of Military History.

Guard Duty, Vietnam, 1967. Stephen Sheldon. Oil on Board, 30" × 24". Courtesy of Army Art Collection, U.S. Army Center of Military History.

SIDE GUNNER IN
A "SLICK" CHOPPER—

Jack O'Hara

Above: Side Gunner in a Slick Chopper, Vietnam, 1969. Jack O'Hara. Pencil, 20" × 25". *Opposite:* Montagnard Civilian Irregular Defense Group Soldier, Vietnam, 1967. Peter Copeland. Watercolor. United States Military personnel commanded non–Americans in combat. Sergeant First Class William M. Bryant, who received the Congressional Medal of Honor, was the officer in charge of a unit which included civilian irregular force members, such as the one pictured to the left, when he was mortally wounded (see citation on page 96). Both courtesy of Army Art Collection, U.S. Army Center of Military History.

Right: Green Beret, Vietnam, 1966. Paul Rickert. Acrylic, 29" × 22⅞".

Below: Helicopter Pick-Up, Vietnam, 1967. Paul Rickert. Tempera on Paper, 9" × 12".

Opposite top: Chow, Lunch Break, Company D, 809 Engineer, Thailand, 1970. Kenneth Grissom. Watercolor on Paper, 22" × 29". *Opposite bottom:* Wade in the Water, Vietnam, 1967. Robert T. Myers. Oil on Canvas, 41" × 46½". All courtesy of Army Art Collection, U.S. Army Center of Military History.

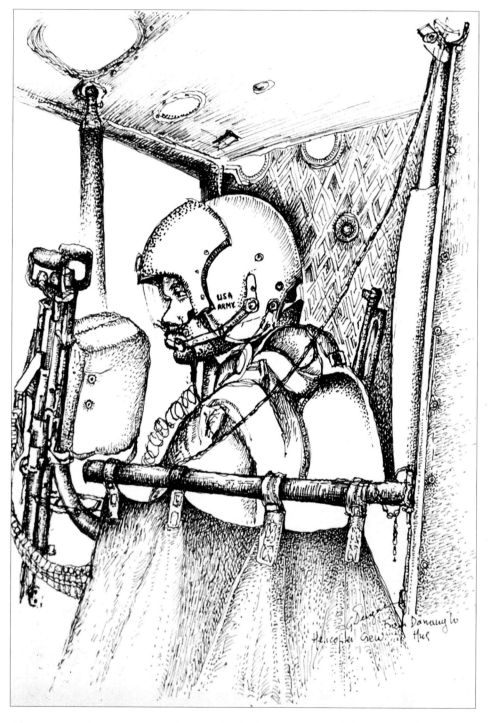

Above: From Danang to Hue, Vietnam, 1967. George Dergalis. Ink, 11⅝" × 9½". *Opposite:* In for Repairs, Long Binh, Vietnam, 1967. Michael Crook. Watercolor, 40" × 30". Both courtesy of Army Art Collection, U.S. Army Center of Military History.

Good Morning, Vietnam. Paul Mac Williams. Oil, 19¼" × 15¼". Courtesy of Army Art Collection, U.S. Army Center of Military History.

Winning Hearts and Minds, Vietnam. Craig Stewart. Oil on Canvas, 34" × 21". Courtesy of Army Art Collection, U.S. Army Center of Military History.

himself to those needing attention, stopping only briefly to care for his own wounds and taking morphine to deaden his pain as the battle raged for some 24 hours. He had treated and saved many lives at the risk of his own until he was ordered evacuated. Joel, a member of Headquarters Company, 1st Battalion (Airborne), 503rd Infantry, 173rd Brigade, was later promoted.

• Sergeant Donald Russell Long, a native of Ohio and a member of Troop C, 1st Squadron, 4th Cavalry, 1st Infantry Division, was in an armored personnel carrier accompanying two units on a reconnaissance mission on June 30, 1966, when they came under heavy fire from a concealed Viet Cong regiment. Sergeant Long left his vehicle in the heat of battle to carry the wounded to evacuation helicopters and to distribute supplies to the men. He then assisted the crew of a disabled carrier to safety and continued to distribute supplies in disregard of his own safety. He rallied the men to press

Easter Sunrise, 1st Cavalry Airmobile Division, Base Camp "English" near Bong Son, Vietnam, 1967. Michael R. Crook. Acrylic, 24" × 30". Courtesy of Army Art collection, U.S. Army Center of Military History.

the enemy. When a grenade landed nearby, he threw himself on it and sacrificed himself to save eight men. Sergeant Long gave his life in the service of his country.

- Platoon Sergeant Matthew Leonard, a native of Eutaw, Alabama, and a member of Company B, 1st Battalion, 16th Infantry, 1st Infantry Division, assumed leadership of his men on February 28, 1967, when the unit was ambushed by a larger enemy force and the platoon leader and other non-commissioned officers were wounded. After the initial attack was repulsed, Leonard set up a defensive area and inspired the men to press the enemy. He was wounded when he went to move a fallen comrade to safety, and wounded a second time when he went to fix a malfunctioning machine gun. He then charged the enemy position and took out the enemy gun crew. In the process, he took several hits from the enemy gunfire. Using a tree as a cover, he continued fighting until he died of his wounds.

• First Lieutenant Ruppert L. Sergeant, a native of Virginia and a member of Company B, 4th Battalion, 9th Infantry, 25th Infantry Division, on March 15, 1967, led a platoon of men to check out a reported enemy location and a weapons cache. They came upon a covered, booby-trapped tunnel entrance which they failed to demolish with hand-grenades. Moving in closer, the Lieutenant and his demolition man knocked out the covered entrance and killed a Viet Cong who had emerged. When the Lieutenant and two of his men approached the entrance, a second Viet Cong tossed two grenades in their midst. Instantly, the Lieutenant fired at the man and then flung himself over the grenades. The two men were slightly injured. First Lieutenant Ruppert L. Sergeant, who was 29 years old, was mortally wounded.

• Staff Sergeant Webster Anderson of Winnsboro, South Carolina, was chief of section of Battery A, 2nd Battalion, 320th Artillery, 101st Airborne Infantry Division, in Tam Ky on October 15, 1967, when his battery was attacked by a North Vietnamese infantry unit. From an exposed position, Anderson directed deadly fire at the approaching enemy. He was severely wounded when two grenades exploded at his feet. From a propped-up position, he directed fire and urged his men to continue the battle. When a third grenade fell near a wounded comrade, Anderson grabbed it. Before he could toss it clear, it exploded and he was wounded again. Refusing medical attention, he exhorted his men to fight until the enemy was repulsed. Webster Anderson, who was 34 years old at the time, was rewarded for his bravery with a promotion and subsequently with the highest honor.

• Captain Riley L. Pitts, a native of Oklahoma, was unit commander of Company C, 2nd Battalion, 27th Infantry, 25th Infantry Division. After his company had cleared the enemy out of its immediate area, on October 31, 1967, Pitts and his company were ordered to reinforce another unit that was under heavy attack. On the way, they came under fire from three directions from a concealed enemy. Using rifle fire and a grenade launcher, the company tried to dislodge the enemy. Unsuccessful, Pitts called in artillery fire and positioned himself on a range where he had a better view of the enemy. He maintained that position and battled the enemy until he was mortally wounded. Captain Riley L. Pitts gave his life in the service of his country.

• Private First Class Clarence Eugene Sasser, a Texan and a medical-aid man of Headquarters Company, 3rd Battalion, 60th Infantry, 90th Infantry Division, was assigned to Company A, which was on a reconnaissance mission on January 10, 1968. The company suddenly came under heavy fire from three sides by a hidden enemy. Sasser immediately began treating the more than 30 soldiers wounded in the first few minutes of the attack. While helping one man to safety, he was hit in the shoulder by exploding rocket fragments. Under heavy enemy fire, he continued to treat the casualties and to search for others. After being wounded in both legs, he dragged himself to administer treatment to others and encouraged still other wounded men to crawl to a safer location. In great pain and suffering from loss of blood, he cared for the wounded for some five hours before being evacuated. Twenty-year-old Clarence Eugene Sasser was subsequently promoted for his courage and bravery.

• Specialist Fifth Class Dwight H. Johnson, a 20-year-old native of Detroit, Michigan, was a tank driver in Company B, 1st Battalion, 69th Armor, 4th Infantry Division. On January 15, 1968, Johnson gave support to his platoon which was engaged in battle with a battalion-size enemy force. When the tank became disabled, Johnson, armed with a pistol, dismounted and took out several enemy soldiers before running out of ammunition. After moving a wounded crewman to safety, he obtained a submachine gun and fought the enemy in close quarters. Out of ammunition a second time, he killed an enemy soldier with the stock end of the gun. After moving a second wounded comrade to safety, he mounted a tank and helped to fire the main gun until it malfunctioned. Dismounting with small arms, he fought the enemy at close range as he made his way back to his disabled tank where, fully exposed, he manned the tank's main gun until the battle abated.

• Sergeant First Class Eugene Ashley, Jr., a 36-year-old native of Wilmington, North Carolina, was a member of Company C, 5th Special Forces Group (Airborne), 1st Special Forces. He was a senior special forces advisor with an assault force assigned to rescue special forces advisors who were pinned down by the enemy. On February 6–7, 1968, Ashley and his team first used explosives and mortar and, when he lost communication with his camp, he called in air and artillery support and organized a small force of friendly natives to charge the enemy. Amid enemy booby traps, automatic weapons, machine guns, and grenade firepower, he led five assaults, which forced the enemy to withdraw. Ashley, who was seriously wounded during the attacks, lost consciousness after the fifth attack. While being carried from the high ground, he was fatally wounded by the enemy artillery. He died a hero's death.

• Staff Sergeant Clifford Chester Sims of Florida was a squad leader of Company D, 2nd Battalion (Airborne), 501st Infantry, 101st Division. On February 21, 1968, Sims and his squad entered a wooded area to attack an enemy force which had been assaulting his company. His squad then was ordered to provide cover for the units of his company to link up with each other. Seeing a pile of burning ammunition, the Sergeant redirected the unit to avoid disaster but not before two of the men were wounded. Still in the wooded area and under heavy fire, the squad ran into a triggered booby trap, whereupon the Sergeant fell on the device. The 25-year-old Staff Sergeant Sims, who had twice moved his men from impending danger, sacrificed himself to save his men.

• Lieutenant Colonel Charles Calvin Rogers, a native of Virginia, was commanding officer of the 1st Battalion, 5th Infantry, 1st Infantry Division. On November 1, 1968, before dawn, an enemy force bombarded his base and a human wave of ground attackers moved into the area. Rogers roused his artillery crewmen and directed their fire at the on-coming enemy. Wounded, Rogers led the attack on a segment of the area where the enemy had penetrated. Wounded a second time, he continued the attack until the enemy was driven out. As Rogers was reinforcing a defensive perimeter, the enemy launched a second wave of human attackers and he rallied his men for a counter attack. At dawn, the enemy made a third attempt to overrun the base. Rogers then directed fire at the oncoming enemy and at one point manned a howitzer that had been inoperative because of casualties. Wounded a third time, he continued to give direction and encouragement until the enemy withdrew. The 39-year-old Rogers survived his wounds.

• First Lieutenant John E. Warren, Jr., a native of Brooklyn, New York, was the platoon leader of Company C, 2nd Battalion (Mechanized), 22nd Infantry, 25th Infantry Division. On January 14, 1969, Warren and his company were on their way to reinforce another unit when they came under attack by an enemy operating from a fortified position. Warren led several of his men through hostile fire to rout the enemy. As he was about to throw a grenade into an enemy bunker, one landed in the midst of his men. Warren fell on the grenade and sacrificed himself to save the lives of others. He died on the battlefield at age 22 in the service of his country.

• Private First Class Garfield M. Langhorn, a 20-year-old native of Virginia, was a radio operator serving with Troop C, 7th Squadron (Airmobile), 17th Cavalry, 1st Aviation Brigade. On January 15, 1969, Langhorn's platoon was assigned the mission to rescue two helicopter pilots who had been shot down by enemy fire. Langhorn provided radio communication with aircraft as the troops searched the dense jungle for the wreckage. After discovering the bodies of the pilots, the men found themselves surrounded by the enemy as they began to move the bodies to a pick-up point. Langhorn then radioed for help and directed the fire of the aircraft. When darkness nullified the effectiveness of aircraft support, the enemy closed in on the men. An enemy grenade fell among the wounded men and Private First Class Langhorn threw himself on it and saved his comrades at the sacrifice of his own life.

• Sergeant First Class William M. Bryant, a native of Georgia, was assigned to Company A, 5th Special Forces Group, 1st Special Forces. On March 24, 1969, Bryant was serving as officer in charge of a civilian irregular defense force when it came under fire. For almost two days of continuous fighting, Bryant gave direction and encouragement to his men. He braved hostile fire to retrieve airdropped supplies. He led a reconnaissance patrol that came under intense enemy fire. He and his men succeeded in forcing the enemy to retreat from the immediate area. Hoping to force a full retreat, Bryant organized a patrol to penetrate the enemy defenses. When the patrol was pinned down and Bryant was severely wounded, he called in helicopter support and directed the fire of the gunship. He then charged the enemy position and destroyed three automatic weapons crews. While he was readying another patrol, he was fatally wounded by a rocket. Sergeant First Class Bryant died on the battlefield at age 33 after more than 30 hours of continuous fighting.

Invasion of Panama
(1989–1990)

In an action dubbed Operation Just Cause, United States troops invaded Panama to overthrow a corrupt dictator and to provide an environment for the election of a democratic government. The operation began in late December 1989 and lasted a little over a month.

Jump Into Night, Torrijos Airport, Panama, 1990. Al Sprague. Oil, 30" × 40". Courtesy of Army Art Collection, U.S. Army Center of Military History.

Air Assault, Tinajitas, Panama, 1990. Al Sprague. Oil, 28" × 40". Courtesy of Army Art Collection, U.S. Army Center of Military History.

Desert Shield–
Persian Gulf War
(1990–1991)

Black men and women were among the American troops sent to the Persian Gulf in an operation designated Desert Shield/Desert Storm to drive out the Iraqi forces that had occupied Kuwait and threatened the security of the region. This war was a United Nations war in which the United States supplied most of the troops.

Bunker Construction, Saudi Arabia, 1991. Peter G. Varisano. Pastel, 24"×18". Courtesy of Army Art Collection, U.S. Army Center of Military History.

101st Ready for It, Saudi Arabia, 1991. Peter G. Varisano. Pastel, 24" × 18". Courtesy of Army Art Collection, U.S. Army Center of Military History.

1st Cavalry, Saudi Arabia, 1991. Peter G. Varisano. Watercolor on Paper, 24" × 28". Courtesy of Army Art Collection, U.S. Army Center of Military History.

24TH INFANTRY DIVISION
MAINTENCE 12/90
P. VARISANO

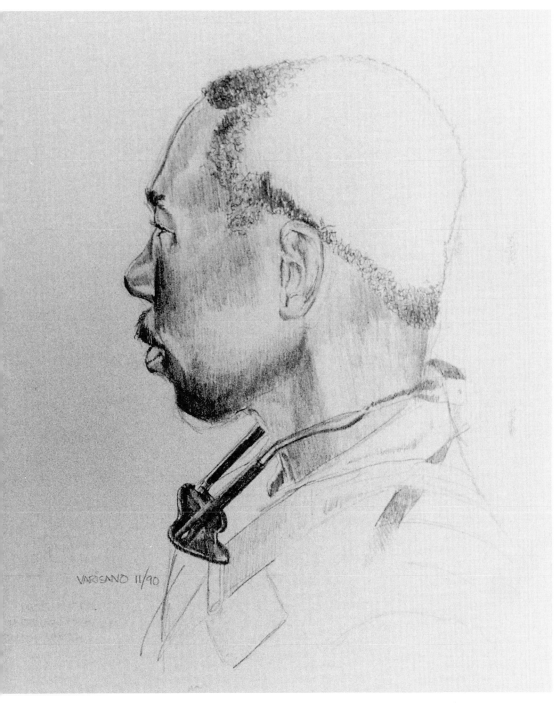

Above: Dust-Off Crew Member (Study), Saudi Arabia, 1990. Peter G. Varisano. Ink. *Opposite:* Maintenance Victory Division, 24th Infantry Soldier, Desert Shield, Saudi Arabia, 1990. Peter Varisano. Ink on paper, 14¾" × 12". Both courtesy of Army Art Collection, U.S. Army Center of Military History.

Above: 24th Infantry Division, Maintenance, Saudi Arabia, 1990. Peter Varisano. Ink on Paper. *Opposite:* Don't Mess with the 101st, Saudi Arabia, 1991. Peter G. Varisano. Watercolor and Pencil on Paper, 30½" × 22½". Both courtesy of Army Art Collection, U.S. Army Center of Military History.

**Water Break, Air Defense Artillery, Saudi Arabia, 1990. Peter G. Varisano. Pencil, 17" × 14".
Courtesy of Army Art Collection, U.S. Army Center of Military History.**

American Hero, Saudi Arabia, 1991. Peter G. Varisano. Watercolor, 24" × 18". Courtesy of Army Art Collection, U.S. Army Center of Military History.

Above: Employee, 24th Infantry Division, Saudi Arabia, 1991. Peter G. Varisano. Pastel, 24"
× 18". *Opposite:* Soldier of the Victory Division Cleans His Fighting Vehicle, Saudi Arabia,
1990. Peter G. Varisano. Ink, 17" × 14". Both courtesy of Army Art Collection, U.S. Army
Center of Military History.

SOLDIER OF THE VICTORY DIVISION
USING AN FIGHTING VEHICLE
24TH INFANTRY DIVISION, OPERATION
DESERT SHIELD.

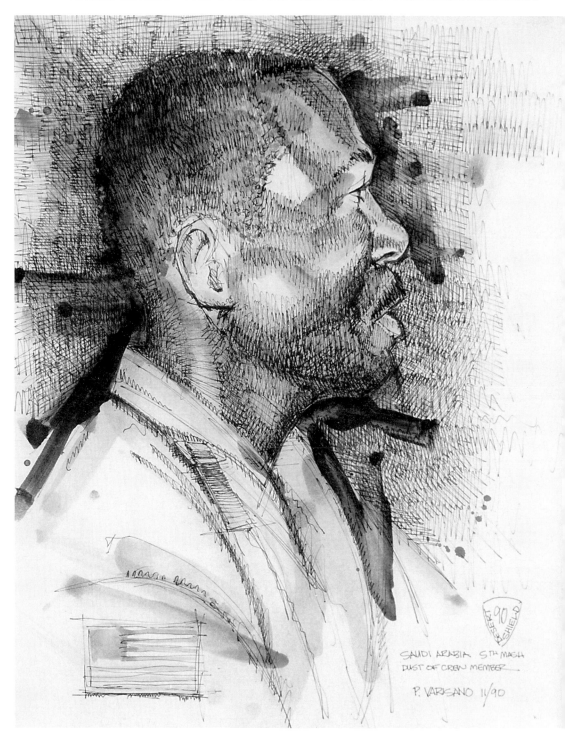

Dust-Off Crew Member, 5th MASH, Saudi Arabia, 1991. Peter G. Varisano. Mixed Media on Paper, 14" × 11". Courtesy of Army Art Collection, U.S. Center of Military History.

One of the Screaming Eagles, Saudi Arabia, 1991. Peter G. Varisano. Pastel, 24" × 18". Courtesy of Army Art Collection, U.S. Army Center of Military History.

Saudi Arabia, 1991. Peter G. Varisano. Pastel, 24" × 18". Courtesy of Army Art Collection, U.S. Army Center of Military History.

Camp Dragon, 18th Airborne, HQS Soldier Helps Construct Framework, Saudi Arabia, 1990. Peter G. Varisano. Pencil on Paper, 17" × 14". Courtesy of Army Art Collection, U.S. Army Center of Military History.

Chaplain Playing Chess with Patient, 5th MASH, Saudi Arabia, 1990. Sieger Hartgers. Watercolor, 22¾" × 30". Courtesy of Army Art Collection, U.S. Army Center of Military History.

Blacks were in the Women's Auxiliary Corps / Women's Army Corps from its beginning in 1942. Some 800 enlisted black women and some 30 black commissioned officers served overseas in England and France during World War II. After the war, women were given permanent status in the military by the Women's Armed Forces Integration Act of 1948. The creation of the all-volunteer force in 1972 resulted in an increase in the enlistment of women in the army. The disestablishment of the Women's Army Corps had the effect of expanding the role of women in the army's mission and activities.

Chaplain Davis, Saudi Arabia, 1991. Peter G. Varisano. Pastel, 24" × 18". Courtesy of Army Art Collection, U.S. Army Center of Military History.

Nurse, 5th MASH, Ad-Dammam, Saudi Arabia, 1990. Sieger Hartgers. Watercolor, 18" × 12". Courtesy of Army Art Collection, U.S. Army Center of Military History.

"First We're Going to Cut It Off, Then We're Going to Kill It" (General Powell). Peter G. Varisano. Pastel, 24" × 18". Courtesy of Army Art Collection, U.S. Army Center of Military History. The title is a quotation from a talk General Colin Powell, chairman of Joint Chiefs of Staff, delivered at a press conference explaining the military plan of action for confronting the Iraqi army.

The first black women to serve in the army were nurses. Eighteen of them were enrolled in the Army Nurse Corps during World War I to deal with a world-wide influenza epidemic, but they were discharged once the epidemic subsided. Some 500 of them served in the corps during World War II. Some of these nurses were posted overseas in Liberia, England, and the Pacific theater of war. The Vietnam War, the creation of an all-volunteer force, and the desegregation of the military provided more opportunities for blacks in the Army Nurse Corps. In 1979, Hazel Winifred Johnson-Brown was appointed Chief of the Army Nurse Corps, the highest ranking position in the corps.

Norman Schwarzkopf, "The Bear," was the commanding general of the military forces in the United Nations operation against Iraq. His deputy was Lieutenant General Calvin A. H. Walker. General Walker, who retired from the army in 1991 after 32 years of active duty, had served in Korea and Vietnam and had a number of other assignments, including the command at Fort Lewis, Washington. At Walker's death in May 1996 at age 58, President William J. Clinton referred to him as one who "achieved prominence as a skilled and disciplined professional and a caring, enthusiastic commander." Clinton added that "his rise from humble beginnings to one of the highest-ranking African Americans in the United States military" was "an inspiration" to others in the service. One of his successors at Fort Lewis stated that Walker "contributed professionalism and competence with a natural warmth and infectious enthusiasm that inspired everyone he met."

Colin L. Powell, at age 52, was the youngest person and first black to have been appointed Chairman of the Joint Chiefs of Staff, and the highest office in

Opposite: The Man of the Year (The Bear), Saudi Arabia, 1991. Peter G. Varisano. Water-color and Pencil on Paper, 30" × 22". Courtesy of Army Art Collection, U.S. Army Center of Military History.

Break Time on Sunday Outside the Mailroom, Saudi Arabia, 1990. Peter G. Varisano. Pastel, 24" × 18". Courtesy of Army Art Collection, U.S. Army Center of Military History.

Playing Baseball, Saudi Arabia, 1991. Sieger Hartgers. Watercolor on Paper, 24" × 18".
Courtesy of Army Art Collection, U.S. Army Center of Military History.

the American military establishment. He served two terms in this office, from October 1989 to September 1993. Powell had begun his army career in 1958 as a second lieutenant after having graduated from college in a Reserve Officer Training Corps program. He was promoted to brigadier general in 1981 and to four-star general in 1986. He retired in 1993.

The first black to hold the rank of general in the regular army was Benjamin O. Davis, Sr. Davis was commissioned second lieutenant in 1901 after having spent several years in the service. He was made a brigadier general (one-star general) in October 1940. He retired in 1948.

Roscoe Robinson, Jr., who graduated from the United States Military Academy at West Point, New York, in 1951, was the first black promoted to the rank of four-star general in the army. Robinson received his fourth star in August 1982. He was in the military for over 34 years.

Hazel Winifred Johnson-Brown, who joined the Army Nurse Corps in 1955, became the first black woman general officer when she was promoted to brigadier general and appointed to the office of Chief of the Army Nurse Corps in September 1979. She was the first black to hold this position, from which she retired in 1983.

Military
Musicians and Bands

Black musicians have been a part of the army from the beginning. The best known of the early black musicians was Barzillai Lew. Lew played and fought in the colonial period and during the American Revolutionary War. He played the drum and fife and fought at Ticonderoga, at Bunker Hill, and with the Twenty-seventh Massachusetts Regiment. Lew was one of a number of black military musicians who were found among the regiments of Massachusetts, New York, New Hampshire, Maryland, North Carolina, South Carolina, Pennsylvania, and Virginia during the Revolutionary War.

The Louisiana Battalion of Free Men of Color, which fought in the War of 1812, had its own band. One of the band's members was Jordan B. Noble, whose "long-roll" of the drum sounded the call to arms of the American soldiers at the approach of the British in the Battle of New Orleans. His drum was heard throughout the action on the battlefield. Noble was a veteran of four wars. He drummed with Louisiana's troops during the Second Seminole War in 1836, in the Mexican War (1846–1948), and with the Louisiana Volunteers for the Union in the Civil War.

During the Civil War, almost every black regiment of the United States Colored Troops had a band or drummers and buglers. This tradition was continued through World War II. The Women's Army Corps had its black band. With the desegregation of the military, black musicians became members of the army's bands in the various units to which they were assigned, including the premier unit, the United States Army Band.

The duties of musicians and bands have been interwoven into the operation of the army. Their music marks the beginning and ending of a soldier's day. The band or drummer, at times assisted by other instrumentalists, helps the soldier on the march to keep his cadence. In the field, the musicians sound the mess call, the sick call, the mail call, the drill call, and the call to duty for various details. In battle, they sound the command of charge and retreat. They are a part

121

Above: Desert Shield Blues, Saudi Arabia, 1991. Peter Varisano. Watercolor, 24"×18". *Opposite:* Saudi Jazz on Sunday, Saudi Arabia, 1991. Peter G. Varisano. Watercolor, 30" × 22". Both courtesy of Army Art Collection, U.S. Army Center of Military History.

of the activities of retreat parades, ceremonial parades, reviews, and presidential inaugurations. They provide inspirational music to the soldier and help to build the soldier's morale. They entertain both the military and the civilian sectors of society. They have been used in recruitment drives and in war bond drives. And, when the soldier is about to be lowered into his final resting place, the bugler sounds the mournful dirge of taps.

In the early days, the military musicians not only sounded the calls and played martial music, but also were an integral part of the combat and support forces. They were combat soldiers, stretcher-bearers, orderlies, and cooks, and performed other duties. Today, most of them have only one duty: to play or sing music. The 50-piece band of the Third Armored Division was on hand to send the soldiers off to the Persian Gulf War.

Peacetime and Peacekeeping Missions

The army's peacetime missions include training recruits, honing skills, participating in training drills, maintaining and testing equipment, going on field exercises and maneuvers, learning and keeping up with technological advances, making strategic and tactical plans, and being prepared to meet domestic and foreign crises with rapid response forces.

The army has peacekeeping forces in Europe, Korea, Kuwait, and elsewhere on foreign soil. Some of these missions have been in place since World War II.

Black Soldier, Florida, 1979. Sieger Hartgers. Pencil, 22" × 17". Courtesy of Army Art Collection, U.S. Army Center of Military History.

125

Black Soldier, Florida, 1979. Sieger Hartgers.
Woodblock Print, 24"×18". Courtesy of Army Art
Collection, U.S. Army Center of Military History.

Black Soldier, Florida, 1979. Sieger Hartgers.
Pencil, 22" × 17". Courtesy of Army Art Collection, U.S. Army Center of Military History.

Urban Assault Training, Saudi Arabia, 1991. Peter G. Varisano. Mixed Media on Paper, 24" × 18". Courtesy of Army Art Collection, U.S. Army Center of Miliary History.

Above: M-60 Squad Gunner, Training Exercise, Fort Lewis, Washington, 1990. Elzie Golden. Oil, 24″×18″. *Opposite:* 82nd Airborne Division Scaling the Wall, Saudi Arabia, 1991. Sieger Hartgers. Watercolor, 24″×18″. Courtesy of Army Art Collection, U.S. Army Center of Military History.

Above: Maintaining, 1985. Jim Butcher. Oil on Canvas, 36" × 33". Courtesy of Army Art Collection, U.S. Army Center of Military History. *Opposite, top:* M-60 Squad Tactics, Training Exercise, Fort Lewis, Washington, 1990. Elzie Golden. Oil, 22" × 28". *Opposite, lower left:* Black G.I. Teletype, Germany, 1972. Robert Winter. Felt Tip, 16" × 12". *Opposite, lower right:* M.P. at University Gate, Somalia. Peter G. Varisano, 1994. Ink, 16¼" × 12½". All courtesy of Army Art Collection, U.S. Army Center of Military History.

Loading Ammunition at Hickam Field, Hawaii, 1946. Gerald W. Ferguson. Watercolor on Board, 8¼" × 5½". Courtesy of Army Art Collection, U.S. Army Center of Military History.

G.I. and Koreans, Korea, 1945. John Pike. Ink and Watercolor, 26½" × 20¾". Courtesy of Army Art Collection, U.S. Army Center of Military History.

Above: Building Cooperation, Honduras. George Banagis, 1993. Watercolor, 17" × 25". *Below:* Providing Food, Florida. Peter G. Varisano, 1993. Watercolor, 18" × 24". Both courtesy of Army Art Collection, U.S. Army Center of Military History.

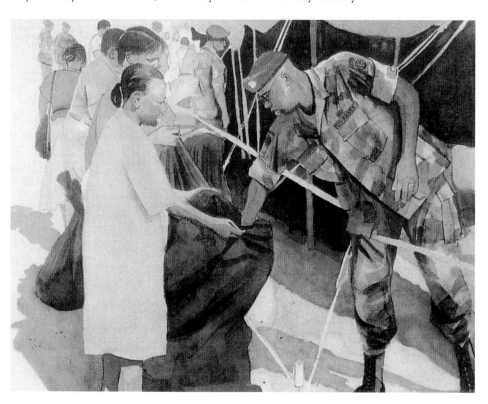

Above: And Don't Forget to Tell Them We're Here, Grafenwohr Range, Germany, 1972. William F. Voiland. Pencil, 24" × 19". *Below:* On Patrol, Czech Border, Germany, 1970. Tom O'Hara. Acrylic on Paper, 20" × 23". Both courtesy of Army Art Collection, U.S. Army Center of Military History.

Appendix 1.
Other Significant Awards,
Commissions and Actions

Restoring to Honor and Pardoning Henry O. Flipper:

In 1976, acting on appeal, the Army Board for Correction of Military Records granted Henry O. Flipper an honorable discharge posthumously. In February 1999, as a result of additional prodding, the President of the United States granted Flipper a full pardon, thereby erasing his military conviction from the record.

Awarding Johnson Chestnut Whittaker a Posthumous Commission:

In July 1995, Johnson Chestnut Whittaker, who was appointed to West Point Military Academy in 1876, was awarded a posthumous commission in the army after years of effort to clear his record. Whittaker had been given the silent treatment by the cadets at the Academy and in 1880 he was found bloodied, bruised, and unconscious in his room. He claimed he was attacked by three of the cadets. The Academy, however, court-martialed him on the charge that he had injured himself to gain sympathy since he was about to fail a course. Whittaker was judged guilty and expelled from the Academy.

Honoring the Davis Family:

In September 1993, the army honored the Andrew J. Davis family of Musella, Georgia, for its sacrifice to the military and the country. Ten of the family's children, all high school graduates, served in the military. Eight of them were in the service during the Persian Gulf War. One, Andrew J. Davis, Jr., was killed during the Vietnam War.

Presenting Lieutenant General Benjamin O. Davis, Jr., a Fourth Star:

In December 1998, Benjamin O. Davis, Jr., received a fourth star, the rank of a full general. Davis was the commanding officer of the 99th

Fighter Squadron of the Tuskegee Airmen and commanding officer of the 332nd Fighter Group during World War Two. He retired from the military in 1970.

Appendix 2.
About the Artists

Samuel E. Alexander, a soldier-artist, received a Bachelor of Fine Arts degree from the Ringlin School of Art in Sarasota, Florida. He was assigned to document events in Vietnam in 1967. (73)*

George Banagis joined the army as an illustrator in 1981 and served as a soldier-artist in Panama and Honduras in 1992. (134)

Romare Bearden was born in 1914 in Charlotte, North Carolina, attended Boston University, and graduated from New York University. He studied at the Art Students League in New York and later under the G.I. Bill at the Sorbonne in Paris. His works are among the permanent collections at the Metropolitan Museum, the Museum of Modern Art, the Hirshhorn Gallery, and the Whitney Museum. President Ronald Reagan bestowed on him the National Medal of Art. He died on March 12, 1988. (15)

Robert Benny was born in Brooklyn, New York, in 1904. He studied at Cooper Union, the Art Students League, and the National Academy of Design in New York. Abbott Laboratories sent him to the Pacific area in 1943 to cover the activities of the Army Medical Corps. After the war, he served as an illustrator for the Air Force and did some paintings for the Marine Corps. He taught at Pratt Institute and at Dutchess College. (58)

Peter Blume was born in Russia and came with his family to the United States in 1911 as a youth. He studied at the Art Students League and received a Guggenheim Fellowship. One of his paintings is in the permanent collection of the Museum of Modern Art. (57)

Aaron Bohrod was born in Chicago in 1907. He studied at the Art Institute of Chicago and the Art Students League. He worked on the Artist Project of the

Numbers in parentheses designate the pages where the artists' works appear.

139

Works Progress Administration. The War Department hired him in 1943 to cover the war activities in the Pacific area. When this program was suspended, *Life* magazine employed him as an artist-correspondent to cover the war activities in Europe. Some of his paintings are in the collections of the Museum of American Art, the Art Institute of Chicago, and the Metropolitan Museum of Art. (53, 54, 55, 59, 61)

Manuel Bromberg was born in Centerville, Iowa, in 1917. He studied at the Cleveland School of Art in Ohio and the Colorado Springs Fine Art Center. He enrolled in the army in 1942 and later was assigned to the War Artist Unit and was sent to Europe. He covered the Normandy invasion and other war activities. After the war, he was awarded a Guggenheim Fellowship in creative painting and later taught at the North Carolina College of Design. (41)

Jim Butcher. Biographical information not in available sources. (130)

Howard Chandler Christy was born in 1873. He studied at the Art Students League with William Merritt Chase. He was an artist-correspondent for *Scribner's* and *Leslie's Weekly* magazines during the Spanish-American War. He made posters to support the war effort during World War II. He taught at Cooper Union, the Chase School, the New York School of Art, and the Art Student League. He died in 1952. (27)

Peter Franklin Copeland was born in New York on July 4, 1922. He was employed by the federal government as an illustrator. As a soldier, he was assigned to the Army Combat Artist Program and was on location in Vietnam from November 20 to December 20, 1967. (77, 84)

Tom Craig was born in California in 1909. He attended Pomona College and the University of California. He studied painting while recuperating from tuberculosis and held a Guggenheim Fellowship in 1941–42. As an employee of *Life* magazine, he was sent to Italy to cover the war effort in 1943–44. After the war, he was an illustrator. (45)

Michael R. Crook, a soldier-artist, was born in 1941 in Lincoln, Nebraska. He had majored in art at Pasadena City College and the Chouinard Art Institute in California. He had been employed doing commercial art and graphics work. In the army, he was assigned to the Combat Artist Program and sent to Vietnam to cover events from February 15 to June 15, 1967. (88, 92)

Richard Dempsey was born in 1909 in Ogden, Utah. He studied at the California School of Arts and Crafts and the Art Students League. He received an award at the Golden Gate Exposition in San Francisco in 1940 and held a Julius Rosenwald Fellowship in 1946. (28)

George Dergalis was born in 1928 in Greece of Russian parentage. He was a prisoner-of-war in Austria during World War II. He studied at the Academia di Belli Arti and the Museum School of Fine Art. He came to the United States in 1951 and served a four-year tour of duty with the Air Force. He was a combat-artist during the Vietnam War. The United States Army Historical Society honored him with the Civilian Merit Award. He served as an artist-in-residence in Columbia for Partners of Americas. (89)

Raymond Desvarreaux. Biographical information not in available sources. (32, 33, 34)

Olin Dows was born in 1904 in New York. He attended Harvard University and Yale University's Department of Fine Art where he studied under E. Savage, E. C. Taylor, and C. K. Chatterton. He enlisted in the army in June 1942 and was one of 12 enlisted men selected to make a pictorial record of the war. He was assigned to Europe. When the army dropped the program, Dows continued to paint. He was discharged from the service in August 1945. (42, 50)

Terry R. Emerson. Biographical information not in available sources. (63, 64)

Gerald W. Ferguson. Biographical information not in available sources. (132)

David Fredenthal was born in 1914 in Detroit, Michigan. He studied at Cranbrook Academy of Art in Bloomfield Hills, Michigan, at the Wicker School of Art in Detroit, and at the Colorado Springs Fine Arts Center. He worked on the Artist's Project of the WPA. He received two Guggenheim Fellowships, one in 1938 and the other in 1939. The War Department hired him as a contract artist during World War II and sent him to the Pacific Theater of Operation. When the army suspended the program, he continued painting under a *Life* magazine contract. He died in 1958. (52)

Albert Gold was born in Philadelphia in 1916. He studied at the Pennsylvania Museum School of Industrial Art. He entered the army in May 1942 and was selected by the War Department Art Advisory Committee and assigned to Europe where he made sketches in England and France. He was discharged from the army in 1945. After the war, he taught at the Philadelphia College of Art. (43, 44, 49)

Elzie Golden attended the School of Visual Arts in New York. He was an illustrator at Fort Rucker, Alabama. He was selected to document the ROTC training program at Fort Lewis, Washington. (128, 131)

Marion Greenwood was born in 1909 in Brooklyn, New York, and studied at the Art Students League and in Paris, France. Working for Abbott Laboratories, Greenwood documented the activities of the Medical Corps at England General Hospital in New Jersey from 1944 to 1945. Some of Greenwood's paintings are in the collections at the Pennsylvania Academy of Fine Arts and the Library of Congress. (55, 56, 57)

Kenneth R. Grissom, a soldier-artist from Jackson, Tennessee, was selected to serve on an army art team, which was on location in Vietnam from October 1970 to January 1971. (86)

John G. Hanlen was born in 1922 in Winfield, Kansas. He studied at the Pennsylvania Academy of Fine Arts and independently with George Harding. The Pennsylvania Academy of Fine Arts and the Library of Congress have some of his paintings in their collections. (47)

James S. Hardy, a soldier-artist, earned a Bachelor of Arts degree in graphics media from San Diego State College in California and did additional study at the Ecole des Beaux Arts, the Sorbonne, and the University of California at Santa Barbara. He was assigned to a combat team and was on location in Vietnam from September 1969 to January 1970. (74)

Sieger Hartgers was born in 1949 in the Netherlands and was a graduate of the Akademie Voor Beeldende Kunsten in the Netherlands. He enrolled in the United States Army in 1972 and had assignments as an illustrator. As a member of the Army Art Program, he

was sent to record training exercises in Florida where he was on location from October 1979 to February 1980. Later, he documented the desert training exercises of the soldiers during Desert Shield. (114, 115, 119, 125, 126, 129)

Joseph Hirsch was born in Philadelphia, Pennsylvania, in 1910. He studied at the Philadelphia Museum of Industrial Arts and privately. He taught at the Chicago Art Institute School and the University of Utah. He held a Guggenheim Fellowship in 1942. Commissioned by Abbott Laboratories, he documented the activities of the Army Medical Corps in Europe. Later, he went to the Pacific war area to record naval activities. He died in 1981. (40)

Joe Jones was born on April 7, 1909, in St. Louis, Missouri. He was a self-taught artist. He worked on the Artist Project of the WPA. At age 27, he had a one-man show in a New York City Gallery. He was awarded a prize by the St. Louis Artist guild in 1928 and another by the Pennsylvania Academy of Fine Arts in 1943. As an artist-correspondent, he recorded military events in Alaska. He is best known for his paintings of wheat fields. (42, 48, 51, 54, 59, 60)

B. Keeler. Biographical information not in available sources. (69)

John D. Kurtz, a soldier-artist, studied at the Pennsylvania Academy of Fine Arts in Philadelphia and the

Academia di Belli Arti in Florence, Italy. He was assigned to a combat artist team and was in Vietnam from February to June 1968 to record events. (78, 79, 81)

Roy E. LaGrone, a designer, illustrator, and painter, studied at Tuskegee in Alabama and the University of Florence in Italy. He was a graduate of Pratt Institute in Brooklyn, New York. He was affiliated with the Society of Illustrators and the Air Force Art Program. (11)

David Lax was born in New York in 1910. He attended the Ethical Culture School in New York and studied under visiting artists. He was drafted into the army in 1942 and assigned to the Fort Dix Special Service Office where he painted murals for the service club. In 1943, he was assigned to the Army Art Program and sent to Europe to document the war. His work dealt mostly with the activities of the Transportation Corps. After the war, Lax taught art at the Dutchess County, (N.Y.) Community College. (45)

Daniel Lopez, a soldier-artist, attended Fresno City College and Fresno State College, both in California. He was assigned to the art program and was on location in Vietnam from August to October 1967. (81)

Ludwig Mactarian was born in New York on January 1, 1908. He was employed on the Artist Project of the WPA. As a serviceman, he was assigned to an engineer unit as an artist-correspondent. His paintings and sculptures may be found in several federal buildings. (55, 67)

Joan Bacchus Maynard was born on August 29, 1928. She studied at the Art Career School in New York, the Fashion Institute of Technology, and the Visual Arts for Film Design. She designed and published Afro-American History Posters in 1961. She was an art instructor. (14)

Barse Miller was born in New York in 1904. He studied at the National Academy of Design in New York and the Pennsylvania Academy of Fine Arts in Philadelphia. In 1942, *Life* commissioned him to sketch the defense areas on the West Coast. He enlisted in the army on July 1, 1943, and served in the combat art section of the Corps of Engineers in the Pacific Theater of Operations until the end of the war. He was affiliated with the National Academy of Design and taught at Queens College until the time of his death on January 22, 1973. (46)

Robert T. Myers, a soldier-artist, had studied at the John McCrady School of Fine and Commercial Art in New Orleans, the Pennsylvania Academy of Fine Art, and in Europe on a scholarship. He was a member of an art team in Vietnam from February 15 to June 15, 1967. Prior to this assignment, Myers had been on active duty in the army for about seven years. (86)

Frank Nicholas, a civilian artist, studied at Hampton University and the Philadelphia School of Design. He has painted and illustrated cards. (24)

Jack O'Hara was born on January 10, 1931. He earned a Bachelor of Fine Art degree from the Massachusetts College of Art in 1956 and a Master of Arts in Education degree from Tufts University in 1957. He also attended New York University and Columbia University. He taught art education at the University of Bridgeport in Connecticut. (80, 85)

Tom O'Hara earned a Bachelor of Fine Arts degree from the Rhode Island School of Design in 1947. He taught at the Massachusetts College of Art. Some of his paintings are in the permanent collections at the USS Constitution Museum at Charlestown, Massachusetts, and the Wiggins portfolio in the Boston Public Library. Some others are displayed at the Air and Space Museum, the United States Marine Corps Historic Museum, and the United States Navy Exhibition Center, all in Washington, D.C. O'Hara served in Vietnam during the war. He died in 1984. (135)

Ronald E. Pepini attended Yale University. He worked as a draftsman and as a technical illustrator. He enlisted in the army in 1965. He was assigned to the Army Exhibit Unit at Cameron Station in Virginia. He was a member of the combat artist team, which was in Vietnam from August to December 1966. (75)

John Pike was born on June 30, 1911. He taught painting and was an illustrator for several magazines including *Redbook, Colliers,* and *Cosmopolitan.* He joined the Army Reserve in 1942 as a pilot and was discharged in 1943 to go into psychological warfare. He received an award in 1942 from the American Watercolor Society. He belonged to the American Watercolor Society and the Illustrators Club. (133)

Jerry Pinkney was born in 1939 in Philadelphia, Pennsylvania. He studied at the Philadelphia Museum College of Art. A designer and illustrator, he was involved in the design work for the Boston National Center of Afro-American Artists. He designed the Harriet Tubman Commemorative Stamp for the United States Postal Service. He received awards from the Society of Illustrators and the Art Directors Show. (9)

Charles Johnson Post was born in New York in 1873. He attended the City College in New York and studied at the Art Students League. He worked as a cartoonist in Philadelphia and New York. He enlisted in a volunteer infantry regiment during the Spanish-American War and went to Cuba where he made sketches of events and later rendered them into oils and watercolors. After the war, he did free-lance writing and illustrating. (29)

William Linzee Prescott was born in New York City in 1917. He studied under various artists and at the Chouinard Art Institute in Los Angeles. He was inducted in the army in 1941 and assigned to the 82nd Airborne Division. He parachuted into Normandy. He was a prisoner-of-war for ten months before escaping. During the Vietnam War, he spent two months on location in 1967 to document the activities. His mural depicting the Normandy Invasion is at the United States Military Academy at West Point. He died in 1981. (76)

Frederic Remington was born in Canton, New York, in 1861. He studied at the Yale School of Art. He traveled to the West and Southwest and made sketches of Indians, Mexicans, life on the range, and especially soldiers. He returned to New York to study at the Art Students League. He won an award at the Paris Exposition in 1889 and was elected to the National Academy of Design in 1891. He was an illustrator for *Harper's* and *Century* magazines. He died in 1909. (19, 20, 21, 22, 23)

Paul Rickert, a native of Philadelphia, Pennsylvania, was a student at the Los Angeles Art Center College of Design. He served as a soldier-artist in Vietnam in 1966. (87)

Robert B. Rigg took some courses at the Art Institute of Chicago but received most of his training from his mother, who was an artist. He won awards for his works in 1961 and 1963. He made a tour to Vietnam in 1963

where he made some sketches and took some notes, which later were the basis for oil paintings. (72)

Paul Sample was born in Louisville, Kentucky, in 1896. He studied at Dartmouth College. He was artist-in-residence at Dartmouth until his retirement. He took a leave-of-absence, was commissioned by *Life* magazine, and was sent to the Pacific area as a war artist-correspondent. His interest was mainly on the operations of the navy. (41, 46)

Kenneth J. Scowcraft was a career soldier who had spent some 18 years in the service before his assignment to Vietnam in 1967 as a member of a combat-artist team. He had studied at the Famous Artist Commercial School and the Army Combat Surveillance School Training Center. He was an illustrator for the army and did freelance painting. (79)

Stephen H. Sheldon was born in 1943. He attended the Art Center College of Design in Los Angeles. He was assigned to a combat artist team, which was on location in Vietnam from February 15 to June 15, 1967. (83)

Sidney Simon was born in Pittsburgh, Pennsylvania, in 1917. He studied at the Carnegie Institute of Technology, the Pennsylvania Academy of Fine Arts, the University of Pennsylvania, and the Albert C. Barnes Foundation. He was inducted in the army in 1941. He was placed in charge of the art project at

Fort Belvoir in Virginia and of the Soldier Mural Project. He helped to organize the army's Art Unit. He was assigned to the commanding general's headquarters in the Pacific as an artist-correspondent. He was discharged from the service in 1946. After the war, he became an instructor and served on the Art Commission of the City of New York. (40)

Lawrence Beale Smith was born in 1909 in Washington, D.C. He was a graduate of the University of Chicago and studied at the Art Institute of Chicago. He produced posters for Abbott Laboratories, which commissioned him in 1944 to document the activities of the Medical Corps in Europe. After the war, he continued his career as an illustrator and painter. (37)

Al Sprague was born in Panama in 1938. He attended American University in Washington, D.C. He was a civilian artist who documented the events of the invasion of Panama. (97, 98)

Harrison Standley was born in San Francisco in 1916. He attended Pomona College in Los Angeles and was a graduate of Stanford. He also studied in Paris. He was inducted in the army in 1941 and assigned as an artist-correspondent to the European Theater of Operations to document the war. After the war, he returned to Paris to continue his art career. (38, 39)

Craig Stewart graduated from the University of Washington with a degree in architecture. A commissioned army officer, he was assigned to a combat artist team, which was on location in Vietnam from August 1969 to January 1970. (146)

Peter G. Varisano, who was born in Pennsylvania in 1956, was essentially self-taught. He enlisted in the army in 1974. He completed the Advanced Visual Information Course at the Signal Corps School at Fort Gordon, Georgia. He later graduated from Norwick University in Vermont. He taught at the Non-commissioned Officers Illustrators School in Colorado. He documented National Guard training in 1989 and Desert Shield in 1990. He has served as artist-in-residence at the Army Art Activity section of the Center of Military History. (99, 100, 101, 102, 103, 104, 105, 106, 107, 108, 109, 110, 111, 112, 113, 114, 116, 117, 118, 122, 123, 127, 130, 131, 134)

William F. Voiland, a soldier-artist, earned a Bachelor of Arts degree from the Washington State University in Pullman, Washington. He was assigned to a combat artist team, which was in Vietnam from October 1972 to February 1973. (82, 135)

Paul Mac Williams. Biographical information not in available sources. (90)

Robert Winter. Biographical information not in available sources. (131)

Bibliography

Christian, Garna L. *Black Soldiers in Jim Crow Texas 1899–1917*. College Station: Texas A&M University Press, 1995.

Cornish, Dudley T. *The Sable Arm: Black Troops in the Union Army, 1861–1865*. New York: W.W. Norton, 1966.

Francis, Charles E. *The Tuskegee Airmen: The Story of the Negro in the United States Air Force*. Boston: Bruce Humphries, 1955.

Franklin, John Hope. *From Slavery to Freedom: A History of Negro Americans*. 5th ed. New York: Alfred A. Knopf, 1980.

Freidel, Frank. *The Splendid Little War*. New York: Dell Publishing Company, 1958

Greene, Robert Ewell. *Black Courage 1775–1783: Documentation of Black Participation in the American Revolution*. Washington, D.C.: National Society of the Daughters of the American Revolution, 1984.

Greene, Robert Ewell. *Black Defenders of America 1775–1973: A Reference and Pictorial History*. Chicago: Johnson Publishing Company, 1974.

Johnson, Charles, Jr. "Formation and Service of New York's 15th Infantry Regiment: Harlem's Hell Fighters during World War I." *Journal of the Afro-American Historical and Genealogical Society*. 12 (1991): 69–79.

Leckie, William H. *The Buffalo Soldiers: A Narrative of the Negro Cavalry in the West*. Norman: University of Oklahoma Press, 1969.

Lee, Ulysses. *The Employment of Negro Troops*. A volume in the Special Studies Series of the U.S. Army in World War II. Washington, D.C.: Government Printing Office, 1966.

MacGregor, Morris J. *Integration of the Armed Forces 1940–1965*. A volume in the Defense Studies Series. Washington, D.C.: Government Printing Office, 1981.

May, Robert E. "Invisible Men: Blacks and the United States Army in the Mexican War." *The Historian*. 49 (August 1987): 463–477

McConnell, Catherine T. and Roland C. "Selected African American Musicians and Bands from Colonial Times through the Civil War." *Journal of the Afro-American Historical* and *Genealogical Society.* 12 (1991): 1–27.

McConnell, Roland C. *Negro Troops in Antebellum Louisiana: A History of the Battalion of Free Men of Color.* Baton Rouge: Louisiana State University Press, 1968.

McPherson, James M. *Marching Toward Freedom: Blacks in the Civil War, 1861–1865.* New York: Alfred A. Knopf, 1967.

Nalty, Bernard C. *Strength for the Fight: A History of Black Americans in the Military.* New York: Free Press, 1986.

Quarles, Benjamin. *The Negro in the American Revolution.* New York: W. W. Norton and Company, 1973.

Quarles, Benjamin. *The Negro in the Civil War.* Boston: Little, Brown and Company, 1953.

United States, Department of Defense. *Black Americans in Defense of our Nation.* Washington, D.C.: Government Printing Office, 1985.

Index

And see Appendix 2, About the Artists, beginning on page 139, for references (in parentheses at the end of each entry) to pages on which each artist's work appears.